Chris C. Pinney, D.V.M.

Vizslas

Everything about Purchase, Care, Nutrition, Grooming, Behavior, and Training

Filled with Full-color Photographs Illustrations by Rick Reason

BARRON'S

Acknowledgments

The author would like to thank Jan Mahood, editor at Barron's Educational Series, Inc. for her insightful advice and guidance during this project. In addition, special thanks go out to Jim and Nancy Gowell, whose passion for the Vizsla further fueled my interest in this breed and prompted me to write this book. Finally, this book is dedicated to Donna Pinney, a wonderful person. She will be sorely missed.

Chris C. Pinney, D.V.M.

© Copyright 1998 by Chris C. Pinney, D.V.M.

All inquiries should be addressed to:
Barron's Educational Series, Inc.
250 Wireless Boulevard
Hauppauge, NY 11788

http://www.barronseduc.com

Library of Congress Catalog Card No. 98-18036

Library of Congress Cataloging-in-Publication Data
Pinney, Chris C.
    Vizslas : everything about purchase, care,
nutrition, grooming, behavior, and training / Chris C.
Pinney ; illustrations by Rick Reason.
        p.   cm.—(A complete pet owner's manual)
    Includes bibliographical references and index.
    ISBN-13: 978-0-7641-0321-6
    ISBN-10: 0-7641-0321-0
    1. Vizsla. I. Title. II. Series.
SF429.V5P55   1998
636.752—dc21   98-18036
                                            CIP

Printed in China

19 18 17 16 15 14 13 12 11

The Author

Chris C. Pinney, D.V.M. is a practicing veterinarian in Schulenburg, Texas. He has written six books about pets, including *German Shorthaired Pointers, Guide to Home Pet Grooming, Caring for Your Older Dog,* and the award-winning *Caring for Your Older Cat,* all published by Barron's Educational Series, Inc.

Photo Credits

Billy Hustace: page 5 top, bottom; 8 top, bottom; 9 bottom; 13 top, bottom; 20; 28 right; 29 left; 40; 45 top, bottom; 48 left, right; 52; 53 left; 56 left; 61 top left, top right, bottom; 65; 68; 69; 72; 77; 81; 97; Zig Leszczynski: page 9 top; 32; 37; 57; Judith E. Strom: page 12 top, bottom; 28 left; 37; 53 right; 100; 101; Paulette Braun: page 25; Mella Panzella: page 29 right; Toni Tucker: page 16; 56 right; 80; 89.

Cover Photos

Toni Tucker: front cover; Barbara Augello: back cover; Tara Darling: inside front cover, inside back cover.

Important Note

This pet owner's guide tells the reader how to buy and care for a Vizsla. The author and the publisher consider it important to point out that the advice given in the book is meant primarily for normally developed puppies from a reputable breeder; that is, dogs of excellent physical health and good temperament.

Anyone who adopts a fully grown Vizsla should be aware that the animal has already formed its basic impressions of human beings. The new owner should watch the dog carefully, including its behavior toward humans, and should meet the previous owner. If the dog comes from a shelter, it may be possible to get some information on the dog's background and peculiarities.

There are dogs that, for whatever reason, behave in an unnatural manner or may even bite. Under no circumstances should a known "biter" or an otherwise ill-tempered dog be adopted or purchased as a pet or show prospect.

Caution is further advised in the association of children with dogs, in meeting with other dogs, and in exercising the dog without a leash.

Even well-behaved and carefully supervised dogs sometimes do damage to someone else's property or cause accidents. It is therefore in the owner's interest to be adequately insured against such eventualities, and we strongly urge all dog owners to purchase a liability policy that covers their dog.

Contents

Preface

In all of my years practicing veterinary medicine, I have yet to encounter a breed quite like the Vizsla. From its humble origins in Central Europe, the Vizsla has firmly entrenched itself within the hearts of a loyal group of followers in this country. Quiet yet determined, gentle yet bold, sensitive yet confident, this dog embodies most of the ideal characteristics one would look for in both a hunter and a pet.

As a hunter, the Vizsla is truly the sportsman's dream. Versatile and effective against a wide variety of game, it clearly fulfills its role as a general utility gundog. As an added benefit, Vizslas make extremely enjoyable pets with seemingly one mission in life—to serve and please their owners. They are also aggressive competitors on the show and trial circuits, providing still another source of thrill and enjoyment for their owners and handlers.

This manual will cover a multitude of topics that will prove quite useful to you as a current or prospective Vizsla owner. A short introduction to the history of the breed and its attributes as a hunter, pet, and competitor will quickly reveal the special nature of the Vizsla. Tips on purchasing a dog, acclimating it to its new home, and training the puppy will help ensure that the relationship between you and your new friend gets off to a positive start. Next, the section on training not only covers basic obedience training, but field training for the hunter as well. Dealing with behavioral challenges, though rare in the Vizsla, will be addressed to make certain the bond that exists between you and your Vizsla remains strong! If you have an interest in breeding your Vizsla, a special chapter has been included to guide you through the process. In addition, preventive health care is covered to provide valuable, practical information designed to help your Vizsla live a long and healthy life. Finally, select diseases and health conditions you should know about are highlighted, including a chapter on caring for your older Vizsla.

The Vizsla is an excellent hunting dog and pet.

What Is a Vizsla?

The Vizsla (pronounced "vish-la") is coveted worldwide as both a refined hunting dog and a loving family pet. Although the number of these dogs registered in the United States is relatively small compared to other pointing breeds, they do have an intensely loyal following who have experienced, first hand, the pleasures and benefits of this remarkable canine companion.

Also known as Hungarian Pointers, Vizslas are classified as general utility gundogs, a group that includes those breeds that locate, point, and retrieve game, all with moderate to excellent efficiency. Among the breeds that share this distinction with Vizslas are German Shorthaired Pointers, Weimaraners, German Wirehaired Pointers, Wirehaired Pointing Griffon's, and Brittanies.

Considered a medium-sized hunter, the Vizsla stands 22 to 24 inches (56–61 cm) at the shoulders and weighs in at 50 to 60 pounds (23–27 kg). It is a slick, shorthaired dog, rusty gold to cinnamon in color, with brown lips, nose, and eyes. A longer tail dock than most pointers contributes to a trim, sleek, racy profile. The Vizsla carries two-thirds of its original tail; the German Shorthaired Pointer carries only one-third.

Vizslas have an aristocratic air, no doubt owing to their close ties with ancestral nobility. Their streamlined yet strong athletic physique results in light-footed, graceful, polished movements that are rarely duplicated by their bulkier peers, such as German Shorthaired Pointers or Weimaraners.

"Vizsla" is a Hungarian word meaning "alert and responsive." Not only do Vizslas exhibit these qualities, they are also highly intelligent and sensitive. Vizslas display an intense desire to please their owners. They readily respond to praise and attention. When these two elements are used as rewards, this breed is relatively easy to train. In fact, Vizslas are so sensitive to their owners' commands that harsh, training methods can stress the dog to the point that training efforts become useless.

A Short History of the Vizsla

It was 895 A.D. and the plains of Hungary shook as barbarian hordes thundered down from the east upon this central European protectorate. The Magyars, a nomadic people who had slowly and methodically migrated over time from the western confines of China to the fringes of eastern

Vizslas are graceful and agile sporting dogs.

Europe, swiftly conquered Hungary and went on to invade other countries on the European continent. Riding small, swift ponies and employing rapid strike tactics, the Magyars were fierce warriors, striking fear into the hearts of the European community at the mere mention of their name. Following a reign of terror that lasted more than 50 years, they were finally defeated in 955 by the German armies united under Otto the Great. Returning to Hungary, the Magyar threat to Europe eventually dissipated as the former warriors embraced Christianity and became civilized, forming an alliance, through royal marriage, with the German states.

The Vizsla first makes its appearance in Magyar tribal art and etchings dating back to the tenth century. Apparently, these dogs were favored companions of the Magyar hunters and falconers. The breed's popularity continued to grow as Hungarian nationality slowly blossomed in the centuries following the subjugation of the Magyars. The Vizsla gained mention in the *Illustrated Vienna Chronicle,* published in 1375 under the direction of the Hungarian king Louis the Great. Excellent at hunting the game birds and large hare that inhabited the vast plains and fertile fields of Hungary, Vizslas were soon viewed as prized possessions by the Hungarian aristocracy, who took it upon themselves to make certain that breed purity and refinement remained unadulterated generation after generation.

In 1825 the Magyar Vizsla Stud Book was officially established to maintain records of pedigrees and to preserve breed standards—descriptions of the ideal Vizsla. It was also about this time that the Vizsla was officially awarded the honor Official Pointing Dog of Hungary. There is certainly no question that this lovable and functional dog had won the heart and respect of the Hungarian people. The

The Vizsla's keen scenting ability makes it difficult for game to hide.

Hungarians always remained protective of their national treasure, and the export of the Vizsla to other countries was routinely discouraged until the end of the nineteenth century.

The breed nearly became extinct during World War I; however, its numbers grew back steadily after the war, and many went to distant shores with Hungarian immigrants. The Vizsla population in Hungary continued to rise during the 1940s, even as another world war ripped through Europe. However, following the war, Hungary fell under Soviet domination. Fueled by the fear of the breed's eradication by the Russians, Vizslas were routinely smuggled out of Hungary into neighboring countries, while many accompanied their owners as they fled Soviet occupation. One such dog that was smuggled into Austria was Panni IV, the foundation dog for a multitude of lines in the United States.

Vizslas began arriving in North America with regularity in the early 1950s. On November 25, 1960, the breed was officially recognized by the American Kennel Club (AKC). This acceptance applied only to the short-haired version of the breed; the wire-haired version, referred to as the "Versatile Uplander," has yet to be

Vizslas exhibit excellent retrieval skills.

recognized by the AKC. It is ironic that even though the Vizsla is renowned for being one of the oldest sporting breeds on record, it is one of the newest sporting breeds to receive recognition by the AKC.

A Versatile Hunter

The Vizsla is an outstanding hunter. Blessed with a refined sense of smell, great eyesight, and a loyal heart, the Vizsla is a formidable opponent to a

The Vizsla is a hard-working, dependable hunting dog.

wide variety of game. Vizslas range much more closely than do German Shorthairs and other pointers, as they like to keep their masters in sight at all times. Hunting at a moderate pace allows them to conserve energy, and, as a result, they can hunt long and hard without becoming winded. This is the perfect hunting dog for the individual on foot who likes a relaxed, leisurely hunt.

Vizslas will hunt meticulously, taking care not to scare up game accidentally. On the other hand, whereas many a hot-blooded pointer has passed by game in the intensity and excitement of the hunt, rarely does this happen to Vizslas. They are ideal for hunting ruffed grouse and woodcock in dense wooded cover. Also, pheasant sitting tight in a corn row or field of tall grass are hard-pressed to fool this hunter and go unnoticed. Vizslas have also been lauded for their performance against quail, especially when hunting small congregations of birds on restricted parcels of land. They are also effective at rooting out rabbits.

Vizslas are not only excellent pointers, but skillful retrievers as well, especially when game has fallen into heavy thicket or wooded areas. They will readily retrieve dove, although it may be difficult for these bundles of energy to wait patiently by their master's side until the next bird falls.

Like most pointers with short coats, Vizslas are excellent swimmers. They won't hesitate to plunge into icy water to retrieve fallen birds, including ducks and geese. However, intense waterfowl hunting in frigid conditions may be too extreme for the average Vizsla, because its short haircoat provides little insulation against cold water.

An Affectionate Pet

Although Vizslas were originally developed for hunting, you don't have to be a hunter to experience the pleasure and companionship that this breed can bring to you. It is true that Vizslas possess a strong desire for the hunt but they seem to be equally contented just being around people. Highly affectionate and loving dogs, they quickly form close bonds with their owners. Loyal to the core, you can count on yours being at your side every chance it gets.

The Vizsla's warm disposition and medium-size frame makes it an excellent choice for households with children. Vizslas are smart and easily trainable—a big plus for the owner who may not have much time to devote to training. Furthermore, their size, sturdy body structure, intense loyalty, and strong instincts, make them excellent watchdogs and protectors of the family. Vizslas are built for endurance and stamina, making them superior exercise partners for walkers and runners.

Still another reason many persons choose Vizslas as pets is that they are relatively low maintenance. They are naturally clean, with short coats that require little grooming. Their teeth seem to accumulate tartar at a slower rate than many breeds; therefore, dental and gum problems are uncommon in this breed. In addition, they have very few psychological problems if provided adequate attention. In general, the Vizsla is a hardy breed, the result of a large and diverse ancestral gene pool nurtured throughout the centuries by Hungarian nobility.

Behavioral Challenges

As with any breed, idiosyncrasies exist that you should be aware of if you are considering the Vizsla as a pet. These dogs are bundles of energy that require multiple daily doses of exercise and attention. Vizslas that aren't allowed to vent their energy are highly prone to boredom and frustration, which in turn can lead to behavioral challenges and compulsive behavior.

Vizslas are known for forming close emotional bonds with their owners.

Also, Vizslas that are housed outdoors away from human companionship are likely to develop bad habits, including nuisance barking, self-mutilation (psychotic chewing and scratching, for example), and digging. As a result, if at all possible, make your Vizsla an indoor dog. This rarely creates a challenge,

Vizslas won't hesitate to take to the water if duty calls on them to do so.

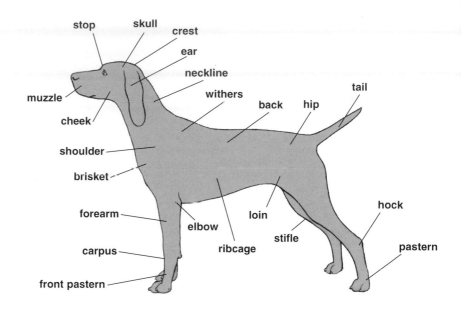

stop   skull   crest
ear
neckline
muzzle   withers   back   hip   tail
cheek
shoulder
brisket
forearm   loin   hock
elbow
carpus   stifle   pastern
ribcage
front pastern

because of the dog's moderate size, short, easy-to-care-for coat, overall cleanliness, training intelligence, and great disposition, but some Vizslas may not like apartments, townhouses, or any other settings that may have only limited space for exercise. Remember: Vizslas need plenty of room to run, play, point, and unleash their instinctive desire for the hunt.

All said, Vizslas make excellent household pets, and the decision to own one for this purpose is a matter of personal preference and circumstance. Rest assured that you will be gaining a loyal, loving companion. Just be sure to give your new companion the attention it deserves and needs on a daily basis.

A Keen Competitor

Competitive events can be fun for you and your Vizsla. You can be sure that the Vizsla's intelligence, looks, and desire to please can make it a formidable competitor! American Kennel Club (AKC) and Field Dog Stud Book

(FDSB) licensed events are regularly held across the country. You can find out about events in your area through your local breeders, veterinarians, trainers, dog clubs, and hunt clubs. You can also contact the AKC and FDSB directly for listings of competitions in your locale. You can also learn about events for your Vizsla via the Internet (see Addresses, page 94).

Dog Shows

Dog shows are competitions sanctioned by the American Kennel Club (AKC) in which dogs are judged on how closely they conform to the ideal standard of temperament and physical characteristics for their particular breed. There are two types of shows. The first, called a specialty show, involves one breed only and is usually held by the breed's national parent club or local regional club. The second type of dog show is the all-breed show in which multiple breeds compete. Specialty shows and all-breed shows are often held in conjunction with one another. The judging in these shows is based on the process of elimination, with the eventual winner being crowned Best of Breed or Best in Show.

Obedience Trials

Another type of AKC event Vizslas can enter is the obedience trial, in which dogs execute a defined group of exercises on command, with their performance scored by judges. Obedience trial scores are not dependent upon conformation or other breed standards, but rather on responsiveness to the handlers' commands.

In tracking tests, dogs are required to follow scents that have been aged over specified distances. These tests are designed to identify the true scenting prowess of each entrant.

Agility

An event that has become quite popular is agility competition, in which dogs are guided by their owners over a course filled with obstacles they must jump over or through, tunnels they must negotiate, and poles they must weave in and out of. These are timed events, measuring agility under pressure. Penalties are assessed if obstacles are missed or knocked down, or if time runs out before the course is finished. As with other types of competitive events, various levels of proficiency receive awards, from the most basic to the most advanced agility talents. Agility meets are sponsored by AKC, Canadian Kennel Club, United States Dog Agility Association, and local clubs.

Field Trials

Field trials are designed to test the ability of a dog to perform the original functions of its breed. For the hunter, these trials offer a chance to extend the thrill of the hunt beyond bird season. They also provide an excellent opportunity to hone hunting skills and

The Vizsla can trace its origins back to the plains of Hungary.

maintain a bird dog in top condition between seasons. Vizslas compete in field trials designated for the pointing breeds. These trials include exercises that test the ability of the dog to scent out game, to go on point, and to remain staunch on that point (see Staunchness on Point. Page 51). Various courses are designed to simulate natural hunting conditions and scenarios, with competing dogs hunting planted game such as quail and pheasant.

Both the AKC and the FDSB sponsor field trials. Among the organizations that conduct field trials falling

A hunter in the field, a fireside snoozer at home.

A Vizsla patiently awaiting its obedience trial.

interested, contact the FDSB or one of these organizations for more information regarding field trials, including dates and locations of events in your area (see Addresses page 94).

Hunting Tests

Hunting tests are noncompetitive sporting events sanctioned by the AKC. For the pointing breeds, these tests first appeared in 1986. Most are organized and run by AKC field trial clubs or by individual breed clubs. Whereas field trials are highly competitive events that pit dog against dog for various titles, hunting tests are more casual, with participants competing against established hunting standards rather than against other participants. The result is a recreational and relaxed event in which there is little pressure to beat the competition. Hunting tests are fun and ideal for the hobbyist who enjoys interacting with fellow bird dog owners.

under FDSB guidelines are the National Shoot-to-Retrieve Association (NSTRA), the National Bird Hunters Association (NBHA), the American Bird Hunters Association (ABHA), and the United States Complete Shooting Dog Association (USCSDA). If you are

Versatility Program

Finally, the Versatility Program, sponsored by the Vizsla Club of America, consists of three tests, all noncompetitive in nature. The first is a conformation test, in which dogs are judged on how well they compare to the official breed standard for the Vizsla. The second test is the obedience test, which, as the name implies, tests a dog's responsiveness and actions to various obedience commands. The third test in the Versatility Program is the field test, in which hunting skills are evaluated. Vizslas that pass all three tests earn the ultimate honor that can be awarded to any Vizsla, the Versatility Certificate.

The Official Breed Standard for the Vizsla

The following is the official breed standard for the Vizsla approved by the Vizsla Club of America December 11, 1995, and effective January 31, 1996.

Training for agility competition.

General Appearance

That of a medium-sized short-coated hunting dog of distinguished appearance and bearing. Robust but rather lightly built; the coat is an attractive solid golden rust. This is a dog of power and drive in the field yet a tractable and affectionate companion in the home. It is strongly emphasized that field conditioned coats, as well as brawny or sinewy muscular condition and honorable scars indicating a working and hunting dog are never to be penalized in this dog. The qualities that make a "dual dog" are always to be appreciated, not deprecated.

Head

Lean and muscular. Skull moderately wide between the ears with a median line down the forehead. Stop between skull and foreface is moderate, not deep. Foreface or muzzle is of equal length or slightly shorter than skull when viewed in profile, should taper gradually from stop to tip of nose. Muzzle square and deep. It must not turn up as in a "dish" face nor should it turn down. Whiskers serve a functional purpose; their removal is permitted but not preferred. Nostrils slightly open. Nose brown. Any other color is faulty. A totally black nose is a disqualification. Ears, thin, silky and proportionately long, with rounded-leather ends, set fairly low and hanging close to cheeks. Jaws are strong with well developed white teeth meeting in a scissors bite. Eyes medium in size and depth of setting, their surrounding tissue covering the whites. Color of the iris should blend with the color of the coat. Yellow or any other color is faulty. Prominent pop-eyes are faulty. Lower eyelids should neither turn in nor out since both conditions allow seeds and dust to irritate the eye. Lips cover the jaws completely but are neither loose nor pendulous.

Dog shows judge how closely the Vizsla conforms to its breed standard.

Neck and Body

Neck strong, smooth and muscular, moderately long, arched and devoid of dewlap, broadening nicely into shoulders which are moderately laid back. This is mandatory to maintain balance with the moderately angulated

Vizslas make great house pets!

hindquarters. Body is strong and well proportioned. Back short. Withers high and the topline slightly rounded over the loin to the set on of the tail. Chest moderately broad and deep reaching down to the elbows. Ribs well-sprung; underline exhibiting a slight tuck-up beneath the loin. Tail set just below the level of the croup, thicker at the root and docked one-third off. Ideally, it should reach to the back of the stifle joint and be carried at or near the horizontal. An undocked tail is faulty.

Forequarters

Shoulder blades proportionately long and wide sloping moderately back and fairly close at the top. Forelegs straight and muscular with elbows close. Feet cat-like, round and compact with toes close. Nails brown and short. Pads thick and tough. Dewclaws, if any, to be removed on front and rear feet. Hare feet are faulty.

Hindquarters

Hind legs have well developed thighs with moderately angulated stifles and hocks in balance with the moderately laid back shoulders. They must be straight as viewed from behind. Too much angulation at the hocks is as faulty as too little. The hocks are let down and parallel to each other.

Coat

Short, smooth, dense and close-lying, without woolly undercoat. A distinctly long coat is a disqualification.

Color

Solid golden rust in different shadings. Solid dark mahogany red and pale yellow are faulty. White on the forechest, preferably as small as possible, and white on the toes are permissible. Solid white extending above the toes or white anywhere else on the dog except the forechest is a dis-

qualification. When viewing the dog from the front, white markings on the forechest must be confined to an area from the top of the sternum to a point between the elbows when the dog is standing naturally. White extending on the shoulders or neck is a disqualification. White due to aging shall not be faulted. Any noticeable area of black in the coat is a serious fault.

Gait

Far reaching, light footed, graceful and smooth. When moving at a fast trot, a properly built dog single tracks.

Size

The ideal male is 22 to 24 inches at the highest point over the shoulder blades. The ideal female is 21 to 23 inches. Because the Vizsla is meant to be a medium-sized hunter, any dog measuring more than 1½ inches over or under these limits must be disqualified.

Temperament

A natural hunter endowed with a good nose and above-average ability to take training. Lively, gentle-mannered, demonstrably affectionate and sensitive though fearless with a well developed protective instinct. Shyness, timidity or nervousness should be penalized.

Disqualifications

Completely black nose.

Solid white extending above the toes or white anywhere else on the dog except the forechest. White extending on the shoulders or neck.

A distinctly long coat.

Any male over 25½ inches, or under 20½ inches and any female over 24½ inches or under 19½ inches at the highest point over the shoulder blades.

Reprinted with the permission of the Vizsla Club of America.

Before You Buy a Vizsla

Before you purchase your new Vizsla, there are several issues that you must first address:

• What function(s) do you want your Vizsla to fulfill? Do you simply want a pet, companion, and/or competitor, or do you want to your dog to be able to hunt?

• Do you want to purchase a puppy or a more mature dog?

• Do you want a male or a female?

• How will this new addition affect other pets currently a part of your household?

• Are you fully aware of the costs and responsibilities associated with Vizsla ownership?

• How much time will you truly be able to devote to your new friend?

• Are you planning to keep your Vizsla indoors or outdoors?

Your Vizsla's Function

If you want a Vizsla simply for companionship, the selection process should be easy.

Vizslas are so affectionate by nature that it's tough to make a wrong choice. To help your dog form an even stronger emotional tie with you, consider limiting your selection to a puppy between eight and twelve weeks old. Puppies in this age group will form strong bonds with individuals who interact in a positive way with them during those crucial weeks (see Socialization page 27).

Showing

If your primary purpose in owning a Vizsla is for the show circuit, you would be wise to closely examine the pedigree of the dog you want to purchase, or, in the absence of a puppy's pedigree, the pedigrees of the parents. Look for AKC championship titles in its recent ancestry, as well as Versatility Certificate (V.C.) designations in the first three generations. If you find these titles, you can be certain that your acquisition is coming from stock. Of course, such a selection will probably come with a higher price tag, but if you are serious about competing, it will no doubt help give you and your dog the edge needed to beat the competition in the show ring.

Hunting

If you are planning to use your dog for hunting, you will need to decide whether you want a fully trained mature hunting dog or an untrained puppy or adolescent. This decision should be influenced by the amount of time you will have available to devote to training, the confidence you have in your ability to do the training, the extent of the actual training and refinement you desire for your dog, and finally, the amount of money you are willing to spend on the process.

Again, purchasing an untrained puppy affords you the opportunity to closely bond with it during its peak socialization period between eight and twelve weeks of age. In addition, you will be able to experience the satisfaction of transforming an inexperienced puppy into a trained bird dog and/or companion. Still another advantage of purchasing an untrained puppy is cost; its price tag is considerably less than that of a partially or fully trained Vizsla.

Be sure you fully understand the costs and responsibilities associated with Vizsla ownership.

American Kennel Club Titles Your Vizsla Can Earn	
AFC	Amateur Field Champion
CH	Champion
DC	Dual Champion
FC	Field Champion
NAFC	National Amateur Field Champion
NFC	National Field Champion
OTCH	Obedience Trial Champion
TRI-CH	Triple Champion
CD	Companion Dog
CDX	Companion Dog Excellent
JH	Junior Hunter
MH	Master Hunter
SH	Senior Hunter
TD	Tracking Dog
TDX	Tracking Dog Excellent
VST	Variable Surface Tracking
CT	Champion Tracker
UD	Utility Dog
UDT	Utility Dog Tracker
UDTX	Utility Dog Tracker Excellent
NA	Novice Agility
OA	Open Agility
AX	Agility Excellent
MX	Master Agility Excellent

The disadvantage of purchasing an untrained puppy, of course, is the time required to mold it into a functional hunter. You also run the risk of making training mistakes, many of which might be avoided by professional training.

The advantages of purchasing a trained dog outweigh any disadvantages that may exist with this option. Purchasing a trained dog can save you anywhere from one to three years, a real benefit if you consider what your time is worth. Your risk of making training mistakes is greatly minimized and the chances of getting a dog with serious behavioral or physical problems is virtually eliminated. In addition, a trained dog offers you immediate gratification and benefits that you can put to use at once.

The biggest disadvantage of purchasing a trained dog is cost. Fully trained Vizslas can cost three to four times as much as untrained pups, depending on the level of training.

Trained Gundogs. There are two types of trained gundogs you can choose from. The first, most experienced level, is the *fully trained* dog. Fully trained Vizslas should be able to remain staunch on point (see Staunchness on Point, page 51), respond to basic obedience commands, and have an inner excitement and zeal for the

Potential Expenses Associated with Owning a Vizsla

Item	One-Time Expense	Annual Expense
Food		$200 to $400
Chew Bones/Treats		$25 to $75
Food/Water Bowls	$5 to $10	
Books/Journals	$10 to $25	
Travel Kennel/Housing	$50 to $150	
Obedience Training Supplies	$25 to $50	
Field Training Equipment	$75 to $300	
Professional Training Classes	$50 to $150	
Routine Vaccinations and Parasite Checks		$50 to $100
Heartworm Preventive Medications		$75 to $100
Grooming Supplies	$15 to $20	
Routine Teeth Cleaning		$50 to $75
Kennel/Boarding Fees (one week)		$50 to $75
City and/or County Registration Fees		$5 to $15
Entry Fees for Competitive Events		$25 to $500
Travel Costs for Competitive Events		$50 to $100
Unexpected Illnesses/Emergencies		$100 to $1,500
Totals	$230 to $705	$630 to $2,940

hunt. Most of these dogs will be one and one-half to three years old at the time of purchase.

The other type of trained dog you can obtain is one that has been *started*. Started dogs will exhibit the same characteristics as fully trained dogs, yet may not exhibit staunchness on point. Most started dogs will be one to two years old at the time of purchase. Neither fully trained nor started gundogs should be expected to be trained in steadiness to wing and shot (the art of remaining stationary when a bird is flushed and shot) or to retrieve.

The type of range restrictions placed on the dog during its training is an important factor worth looking into. As a rule, the majority of Vizslas are trained to be close to medium range workers; that is, they tend to hunt out in front of their owners at a distance of anywhere from 5 to 200 yards (4.6–183 m), but be sure you find out the range at which your dog was trained.

Male or Female?

Deciding which sex your new Vizsla should be is strictly a matter of personal preference; both male and female Vizslas make excellent pets. Male dogs are thought to be more spirited and protective; females are generally regarded as more affectionate and

Be sure food and water bowls are sturdy enough not to tip over easily.

trainable. These qualities will vary in individual dogs, however, and will be influenced by such factors as genetics, training, and neutering. As hunters, both sexes offer distinct advantages and disadvantages; for example, male Vizslas are believed to exhibit extra drive and stamina during the hunt, whereas females have the reputation of being more biddable (easily trained), loving, and responsive. One definite factor you will have to contend with if you choose a female is her heat cycle. On the average, female Vizslas come into heat twice yearly, and there is always a chance that a heat cycle could coincide with hunting season or competitions. Although she still will hunt, hormonal influences during this time could adversely affect her performance. In addition, she obviously could not be hunted or competed beside male dogs during her heat cycle without causing a distraction. Of course, if you are not planning on breeding her, having her spayed will eliminate these concerns altogether.

Other Household Pets

Do you currently have other pets living in your house? Jealousies and incompatibilities could arise that need to be anticipated before your new Vizsla is brought home. If you own a cat, how does it behave around dogs?

Still another important question to ask yourself if you already own another dog is, "Has it been properly socialized to other dogs?" If the dog you already have at home attacks anything that barks or moves on four legs, you may have a challenge on your hands when you bring your Vizsla home. Unsocialized dogs (and even some that *are* socialized) may refuse to allow another canine into their territory without a fight.

Finally, use caution when allowing your new hunter around pet hamsters, gerbils, guinea pigs, rabbits, and birds. It can easily mistake these pets for game, with disastrous consequences!

When first allowing your new Vizsla to interact with your existing pets, closely supervise all interactions and keep them under 15 minutes for the first several days. Gradually increasing the amount of time allowed for supervised interaction over the next two to three weeks will help complete a smooth acceptance into the family.

Note: Most fights will break out over a food bowl, so never allow new and existing dogs in a household to eat in the same room until a bond has been established between them.

Costs and Responsibilities

The decision to bring a new Vizsla into your home carries with it costs and responsibilities (other than the purchase price) that you may or may not have expected. Many of these are related to basic dog equipment, feeding, and health maintenance; others to extracurricular activities such as competitive events, advanced training, and travel (see Potential Expenses Associated with Owning a Vizsla, page 17).

For instance, if you are going to be entering your Vizsla in competitive events, be aware that there will be entry fees and travel expenses related to these activities. Also, advanced obedience and field training is costly;

ask your local club for several recommendations for trainers, then call these trainers and compare prices. Consider having the kennel or breeder from whom you bought your dog conduct this advanced training. You may get a price break since you purchased your dog from him or her.

Finally, if you travel often on your job or with your family, you may find yourself accumulating some pretty hefty boarding bills for your Vizsla. Plan on budgeting for such expenses throughout the year for those times when you won't be able to take your dog with you. Another area for which you should set aside money every month is your pet's medical fund. Apart from routine checkups and vaccinations, your Vizsla may need other procedures performed periodically as well, including teeth cleaning and blood screenings. There might be unexpected injuries or illnesses. It is certainly wise to put some funds aside each month as an insurance policy rather than be caught off guard financially when some unexpected health challenge involving your Vizsla pops up.

Spending Time with Your Vizsla

This breed needs a great deal of attention and interaction. If you are crunched for time, be prepared to make time in your schedule for activities with your Vizsla just as you would other important appointments. The majority of these activities should involve movement, and lots of it—exercise, obedience work, field work, retrieval training, and so on. Two excellent times are in the morning before you go to work, and when you arrive home in the evening. Doting on your dog and wearing it out with exercise before you leave for the job should make your exit less stressful for your friend. In addition, you can well imagine the frame of mind a Vizsla is in after having been deprived

of its owner's presence for eight hours or more. As a result, devoting time to your dog as soon as you can after getting home from work will make your Vizsla—and you—very happy.

Don't forget the few minutes of quality time you'll need to spend each day simply petting your dog and talking softly to it. Be prepared to take full advantage of one of the greatest benefits of dog ownership—strengthening the emotional bond between pet and owner. The therapeutic benefit of such an action is not only important for your dog's mental health, but for yours as well.

Housing Your Vizsla

Since Vizslas require lots of human contact, plan on making yours a house dog. A properly trained Vizsla makes an excellent indoor dog. In addition, Vizslas housed indoors tend to be more emotionally stable than those isolated outside, away from owner contact.

When housing your Vizsla indoors, designate a special area (a room or a partitioned section in the room, a bed, pen, or crate) that it can claim as its den and sleeping quarters. When your puppy first comes home, place it in this area. Allow the pup 15 minutes or so to examine the area before allowing it into the rest of the home. Make the experience a pleasurable one. Praise your puppy enthusiastically and offer it some food to eat. Get it to associate that location with pleasure. If you are bringing a newly purchased adult Vizsla into the house, be sure to ask the breeder where the dog slept while in his or her care and consider allowing your dog access to a similar location in your house.

Indoors

When keeping a dog (and especially a puppy) indoors, there are a number of safety measures you should implement in your house to ensure an accident-free environment for your pet.

Plan on spending quality time with your Vizsla each and every day.

• Keep all plants out of reach. Puppies love to chew on plants, and could harm themselves if they ingest a poisonous variety. Ask your veterinarian for a list of poisonous plants.
• Keep all electrical cords well out of reach. This may mean banishing your playful pet from certain areas of the house, but this is a minor inconvenience compared to a potentially fatal accident. Puppies love to chew, and electrical cords are very appetizing to unrefined tastes.
• Keep everything that's not a dog toy picked up, including spare change. Pennies contain high levels of zinc, and could cause a severe gastroenteritis if swallowed.

Remember: Puppies explore their environments with their mouths and will pick up (and often eat) anything.

Obviously, you'll want to confine your Vizsla to noncarpeted floors until it's properly housetrained. Even so-called "stain-resistant" carpets may not uphold this claim after repeated bombardments.

Outdoors

There will undoubtedly be special situations that do not allow for the indoor dwelling of a grown dog. In these instances, consider your pet's comfort and well-being in providing outdoor accommodations. Remember that dogs get hot and cold just as we do, and, when housed outdoors, need to be provided a means of protection against extremes in the weather. Your Vizsla is entitled to a sturdy, well-insulated shelter, which should be positioned in a relatively shady area of the yard, and elevated a few inches off the ground on bricks or wood to prevent flooding in the event of a rainstorm. Ideally, the shelter should have a short, enclosed porch that leads into the main house. This will help keep wind drafts from penetrating into the main living area, which should be large enough to allow your dog to turn around in comfortably, yet confined enough to provide a sense of security and to concentrate warmth in cold weather. Finally, a ramp should be included to allow your dog easy access into its abode, especially after a long day's hunt.

The House. If you are inclined to build the house yourself, select sturdy building materials, remembering that they must withstand constant punishment from teeth and claws. If you use fiberglass insulation, make certain it remains well-contained and sealed within the walls and roof, since such material can cause the dog severe gastrointestinal upset if swallowed.

The Pen. If you plan on further confining your dog to a pen or run, use smooth concrete or quarry tile as flooring for the enclosure. Though such surfaces may not be the most comfortable for your pet, they are the most sanitary and easy to clean.

Floors made of grass, sand, pebbles, or just plain dirt only serve to trap and accumulate filth and disease, and should be avoided.

The Fence. The fence surrounding the enclosure should be made of wire chain link and be tall enough to prevent an acrobatic exit. Exposed metal points from the chain links at the top of the fencing material should not be allowed to extend above the metal support bar in order to prevent injuries if your dog tries to jump. The same rule applies for the bottom perimeter of the fence, in case your dog tries to squeeze its way out from down under.

Keep in mind that daily interaction and attention given to a Vizsla housed outdoors is essential to its mental and physical health, especially for the dog that was raised indoors as a puppy. As a responsible Vizsla owner, be sure to devote plenty of time out of your busy schedule to accommodate these needs.

Finding a Vizsla

Once you are fully convinced that the Vizsla is the right breed for you, it's time to start your search. A great place to start is your local or national breed association. It should be able to direct you to a number of reputable breeders or trainers who may have the Vizsla you are looking for. Dog trainers, hunting clubs, and shooting preserves can provide a wealth of information as well, and most sporting journals, hunting magazines, and dog-related publications are full of information and advertisements for both trained and untrained Vizslas of all ages. Once you have found your source, gather as many references as you can from people who have purchased puppies originating from the breeding pair your puppy will come from, and call them all.

Before committing to a purchase, be sure to request a copy of the dog's pedigree and its parents' AKC registra-tion papers. If at all possible, go to the breeder's location to observe and interact with the puppy or dog in its original environment. Always perform a prepurchase evaluation (see HOW-TO: Performing a Prepurchase Evaluation page 22). It is a good idea to have your veterinarian examine the dog before you make a commitment. Most breeders and trainers will allow this, but they may not be willing to pay for it. Regardless of who has to pay, it is money well spent. While at the veterinarian's, have him or her check the puppy's deworming and vaccination record to make sure everything is current.

Before signing a sales contract, always request that a 30-day trial period be incorporated into the contract so that you can test your dog's personality and temperament, not to mention its hunting skills if it is already trained. If you are planning on purchasing a trained dog, coordinate your purchase to coincide as closely with hunting season as possible so that you can evaluate your new dog's performance immediately. Reputable breeders and trainers stand behind the quality of their dogs and rarely have a problem with such an arrangement. If the dog proves to be unsatisfactory for any reason, most breeders and trainers will allow you to return it for a full refund, no questions asked. Nevertheless, be sure this is stated in the contract.

Upon the purchase of your dog, its breeder will give you an AKC registration application, which has been partially filled out with information about your dog's characteristics, pedigree, and date of birth. Finish filling out this form with your name, address, and the name you would like your dog registered under, and mail it and the application fee directly to the American Kennel Club. The AKC will then send you an official registration certificate for your safekeeping.

How-to:
Performing a Prepurchase Evaluation

Check the dog's mouth for missing teeth and gum problems.

Once you think you've finally found your perfect Vizsla companion, now what? For starters, you want to be sure you are getting a healthy puppy. Begin by inquiring about the dog's vaccination and deworming history. You might be told that all of the shots and dewormings have been given. While this may be true, don't hesitate to ask for, in writing, the dates and names of products used. This list can then be reviewed for completeness and accuracy by your veterinarian.

Next, perform your own prepurchase exam. It is easy to do and will help eliminate many problems that might otherwise elude the untrained eye. Focus on the following areas:

Environment
To begin, take note of the environment in which the puppy or dog is being kept.
• Does it look and smell clean, or is it dirty, with urine and feces lying around? If the latter is true, you should begin to question the integrity of the seller.
• Observe all of the pups and dogs in the litter or group. Do any appear sickly, depressed, or otherwise unhealthy? An infectious disease can spread rapidly through such a congregation of canines.

Attitude
Now focus your attention on the actual candidate.
• Does it appear active and healthy, or is it lethargic and depressed?

• Are breathing problems evident?
• Does it seem friendly and outgoing to people and to the other dogs in the group, or does it seem shy and introverted? Vizslas destined to be good pets should take an instant fancy to people, and should show this affection outwardly.
• Avoid those individuals with overbearing and domineering personalities. Observe how your favorite treats other members of its group. Domineering personalities are usually quite evident. As a general rule, choose one that is middle of the road: not too dominant, yet not too shy.

Skin and Coat
Once attitude and personality have been evaluated, check out the skin and coat. Are any fleas or ticks present? How about any hair loss, scabs, or signs of infection? These could be indicators of common communicable skin diseases such as mange or ringworm, both of

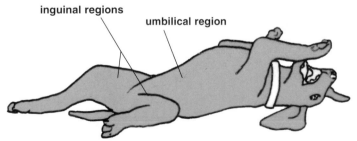

inguinal regions

umbilical region

Regions where hernias can be found in a puppy.

which can be contagious to people.

Lumps, Bumps, or Swellings

Run your hands over the umbilical and inguinal areas (where the inner thighs connect with the abdominal wall) and feel for any soft, fluctuant masses; these may indicate that there is a hernia. Umbilical hernias rarely cause a problem but inguinal hernias can be serious. Run your hands over the entire body surface, feeling for other types of lumps and bumps. Enlarged lymph nodes located in the areas of the neck, shoulder, inner thigh, and knee usually indicate an active infection.

Abdomen

Does the belly seem distended? If so, it could be full of food, or it could be full of worms. Find out when the puppy last ate. If the distension lasts longer than two hours following a meal, worms are probably to blame for the abdominal swelling. Check beneath the tail, looking for tapeworm segments. These will appear as white,

Feel the abdomen for lumps and bumps.

motile wormlike structures or, if dried out, brown grains of rice. Also look for evidence of diarrhea. Soiling on and around the anal area should tip you off to this condition.

Head Region

• Using your eyes and nose, check the ears for discharges or strong odors (usually a sign of infection).
• Both eyes should be free of matter, with no cloudiness or redness.
• Compare both eyes, making sure the pupils are the same size.

• Look at the nose, noting any discharges or crustiness.
• Look into the mouth. The gums should be pink; if whitish, the puppy could be anemic.
• Notice any severe underbites, overbites, or missing teeth.
• Look at the roof of the mouth. In young puppies, a cleft palate is a serious birth defect, and unless it is surgically corrected, it will lead to secondary aspiration pneumonia and death.

Other Anatomical Considerations

• Observe leg conformation, and the way the puppy or dog walks and runs. Any obvious deformities or lameness should be noted.
• In male dogs, check that the testicles have descended. Both testicles should be present at birth; if they aren't, be prepared to have your Vizsla neutered at a later date, not only for health reasons, but also to prevent the passage of this inheritable trait to future generations. Because of its genetic origin, this condition is a disqualification from the show ring.

Raising Your Vizsla

Welcoming Your Puppy

When you purchase a puppy, its first encounters with your family members are important. Be sure that the initial introductions—either with children or other adults in the family—turn out to be positive ones. Carefully supervise children-pet interactions, and stress to the children the importance of gentle play and handling. Instruct your children and other adults in the proper way to pick up and hold the new puppy: Dogs should not be picked up only by the front legs or by the neck; the entire body should be picked up as one unit, with the hind end supported, not left dangling in midair.

If they had it their way, most children, and some adults for that matter, would love to play with a new puppy 24 hours a day. You need to emphasize the importance of rest times for your new puppy after periods of play, and lay down strict ground rules against disturbing it while it is in its special room or bed. It is fine to play with your puppy, but overt roughhousing should be avoided. If a play session progresses from a friendly romp to an all-out frontal assault, end it immediately. Your puppy needs to learn how to keep its activity level to an intensity that is socially acceptable.

You also need to redirect chewing activity. It's perfectly natural for a puppy to want to explore its environment and express itself with its mouth. During play there will be times when it will bite and nip; when this occurs, simply and firmly say "No," and provide a chew toy as a substitute. Remember that if you are planning to train a hunter, avoid playing tug-of-war with your puppy. Doing so only creates a dog that has a "hard mouth" when it comes to retrieving birds.

Toys

The toys that you purchase for your new Vizsla to play with should be nylon, rawhide, or hard rubber. Of the three, the first is most desirable, since it is most easily digestible if swallowed. Rawhide is fine if the dog takes its time and chews slowly. For gulpers that don't have time for chewing, avoid giving rawhide, which can cause serious stomach upset and sometimes intestinal blockages. Also, some dogs have difficulty differentiating rawhide from leather, which could put your new pair of shoes in serious jeopardy. Rubber chew toys should be solid so they're not easily ripped apart by sharp puppy teeth. Avoid chew toys containing plastic "squeaks" that can be easily extracted by most dogs, and can cause choking. Regardless of the type of chew toy you pick, choose it as carefully as you would a toy for a child.

Most important, be sure the decision has been made as to who in the family is going to be responsible for daily feedings, brushing, dental care, exercise training, and other dog-related jobs. Remember: If it doesn't get assigned, guess who will end up doing it all?

Naming Your Vizsla

If you are purchasing an adolescent or adult dog, you'll want to keep the name that was used in its training by the previous owners; however, for new puppies, the task of naming the pup will fall upon you. Naming your new addition should be fun and should involve the entire family. You can find entire books dedicated to choosing the right name for your dog. Stick to names having two syllables; this will allow your dog easy differentiation between its name and those one-syllable commands that it will learn during obedience and field training. You can further set its name apart by adding a vowel sound to the end of it. Be consistent when using the name. If you name your dog "Bella," don't shorten it on occasion to "Bell." You'll only confuse your pet.

House-Training a New Puppy

House-training your Vizsla puppy should be started immediately, preferably before the puppy has reached 12 weeks. The reason: When a pup is 8 to 12 weeks old, its mind is wide open to suggestions, and you can house-train it quite quickly. If you are purchasing an older dog, hopefully this training task has been taken care of. Be sure to verify this before signing on the dotted line.

You must be willing to devote some quality time to house-training. Recognize that puppies have four fairly predictable elimination times:
1. after waking
2. after eating
3. after exercising, and
4. just before retiring for the night.

Make a concerted effort to take your puppy outside during these times, and every three to four hours in between. When you suspect that it has to go out, take it outside and set it down. If it eliminates, praise it lavishly and then take it immediately back inside. By doing so, you'll help the pup associate the act with the location. If a minute passes and your pup hasn't eliminated, take it back inside; don't leave it outside to play or roam. Pup-pies trained this way soon realize that their primary reason for being outside is to eliminate, not to play.

What happens if you catch your puppy in mid-act? If this is the case, rush the pup outside. It may finish what it started before you get outside, but don't be upset. Again, heap praise on your puppy then immediately bring it back inside. If you happen to miss an accident altogether, don't worry. If you saw it happen, a verbal negative reinforcement is indicated; however, if you didn't see it happen, *do nothing!* Simply try to be more attentive next time.

To assist in your training efforts, establish a regular feeding schedule for your new puppy. Feed it no more than twice daily, and take it outside after it finishes each meal. It is preferable to feed the evening portion before 6:00 P.M. This will help reduce the number of overnight accidents.

Also, to help prevent accidents, keep your puppy in a confined area at night. This area should be puppy-proofed, and have a type of floor that won't be damaged if a slipup occurs. Set up a puppy gate in the doorway of a utility

Provide your Vizsla pup with plenty of safe toys.

Be sure to teach your child the correct way to hold a puppy.

room, bathroom, or kitchen. If an accident occurs during the night or while you are away, don't get upset. As your training sessions progress, you'll find that this will occur less and less often. A natural instinct of any canine is to keep its "den" clean. Combined with proper house-training efforts on your part, your puppy's instinct will help make your training efforts a success.

Finally, if you find yourself having to clean up an accident, use an odor neutralizer instead of a deodorizer on the area in question. These are available at most pet stores and will, in most cases, effectively eliminate any lingering scents that may lure your pet back to the same spot. Avoid using ammonia-based cleaners, since ammonia is a normal component of canine urine and such cleaners might serve to attract, rather than repel, repeat offenders.

Understanding Vizsla Behavior

Have you ever wondered why your Vizsla acts and reacts the way it does in the field and at home? Have you ever been faced with a canine behavior problem and didn't quite know how to respond to it? Are dogs truly color-blind? How do you teach an old dog new tricks? The answers to these and other questions can be provided from a basic understanding of canine behavior.

How Vizslas Look at Life

As you can guess, dogs perceive their world differently than we do. This is vital to remember, especially when training them, since in our own perception we may not completely understand certain responses and behaviors that we see in them. By learning how our dogs perceive their world with their senses, however, the reasons become clearer.

The visual acuity of the dog has been compared to that of a human's at sunset; they see only generalized forms rather than distinct images or features. Have you ever worn a new hat or sunglasses with your dog, then have it back away or bark in apprehension? Because you changed your features, it was initially unable to recognize you visually; only your scent gave you away. Some dogs exhibit a high degree of nervousness and even aggressiveness at Halloween. The reason: all those generalized forms (costumes) it has never seen before running from house to house yelling "Trick or treat."

Contrary to popular belief, dogs are not totally color-blind; in fact, the canine eye possesses all the structures necessary for it to perceive its world in color, but whether the dog takes full advantage of this is still a matter of speculation. It seems, however, that since the sense of sight is not as vital to most dogs as the sense of smell, there may be little need for color perception.

The sense of smell is by far the most important sense for a dog, especially the hunter. The brain of the dog has almost 10 times more area devoted to smell than does the human brain. The excellent tracking skills of the Vizsla arise from its ability to detect distinct volatile fatty acids or blood on the skin surface of game or on surfaces with which the game has come in contact. In fact, the canine nose is so acute that it's nearly impossible for a scent to escape it. This allows a dog to use its nose as a homing device, trailing a weak scent over a considerable distance until it gets stronger and stronger and finally leads the hunter to the quarry.

The sense of hearing in the average dog is much more fine-tuned than that in a human, allowing it to detect much higher sound pitches at a wider range of frequencies. The upper range of canine hearing is thought to be around 47,000 cycles per second, almost 30,000 cycles per second higher than that for people. "Silent" dog whistles are based on this principle. They emit a pitch just above human hearing range but well within that of the dog. Since the long, pendulous earflaps of the Vizsla may muffle this pitch at a distance, don't rely upon silent whistles for field training.

Taste. Have you ever wondered why some dogs, when fed table scraps, become incessant beggars? The answer lies in their tongue, which contains a high proportion of taste buds that respond to sugars and certain sweet amino acids. In essence, your Vizsla can quickly develop a sweet tooth if fed improperly. Some dogs will even go so far as to refuse well-balanced rations for the sweeter junk food. The ramifications of this regarding the health and performance of your hunter are obvious. To prevent bad habits from forming, avoid the temptation to consistently sneak your pal snacks between meals.

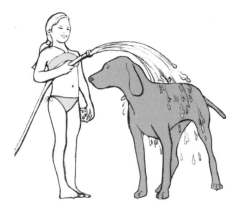

Caring for your Vizsla should be a family affair.

How Vizslas Learn

The most basic type of learning by Vizslas is *habituation,* which is characterized by a diminishing response to a repeated stimulus over time. Teaching a Vizsla to remain calm in the face of gunfire is a classic example of this type of learning put to practical use. A second type of learning that influences behavior is called *associative learning,* in which the dog creates links between two or more different types of actions, results, and/or stimuli; for example, rewards given for desired behavior invoke this type of learning, creating a strong pleasurable link with the behavior in question, and greatly increasing the chances that your dog will repeat the behavior.

Socialization

Socialization, or species imprintation, is also thought to be a form of associative learning; however, it undoubtedly involves more complex learning patterns as well, as evidenced by its often irreversible nature.

There is no doubt that the most important time in the life of your Vizsla puppy is between the ages of 3 and 12 weeks. During this short time, your

The Vizsla has an acute sense of smell.

Vizslas are among the most intelligent of all the sporting breeds.

young hunter will learn who it is, who you are, and who and what all those other living, moving beings surrounding it are as well. If, for some reason, a puppy fails to be properly introduced to members of its own species or to other species—including children—during this time, there is a good chance that it will not recognize these individuals for who they are and may even show aggressiveness toward them. For instance, dogs intended for breeding purposes must be properly socialized to members of their own species if they are to be expected to breed easily with one of these members. Good examples of dogs not properly socialized include those that may show extreme aggressiveness only to men or to children.

Dogs see people as two species: big people and little people. As a result, although a dog may recognize an adult as the one who feeds and commands it, it may not recognize a

small toddler as one who also commands respect if it has never been properly socialized to small children. Some dogs aren't fit for any type of human interaction at all; these dogs have absolutely no socialization whatsoever and could pose a threat to humans. Fortunately, Vizslas rarely fall into this category.

Another good example of the socialization principle is the relationship between dogs and cats. Dogs and cats that grow up together from the start may be the best of buddies; those that don't may exhibit marked animosity toward one another.

Improper or negative socialization is even worse than no socialization at all. Any traumatic experience or physical punishment that occurs between 8 and 12 weeks could permanently scar a dog's personality to a specific group or species for life; for instance, many dogs that fear men were actually

A well-behaved dog is a good companion.

Nuisance barking can be caused by separation anxiety.

abused by a member of this sex during their critical socialization time. This is one reason why all physical punishment should be avoided during this time in your puppy's life—such activity could damage the pup's relationship with the punisher for life.

Whenever purchasing a Vizsla older than 12 weeks, question the seller about the puppy's socialization experiences and the specific steps the seller took to ensure that proper socialization took place. If you don't, you have no way of knowing whether or not proper socialization has taken place, and you may be faced with behavior problems or poor field performance in the future.

Behavioral Problems

Nothing can do more to endanger the bond you share with your Vizsla than behavior problems. The bad news is that addressing behavior

problems takes time and effort on your part; the good news is that most can be brought under control through the use of special techniques and/or therapy. By allowing your veterinarian to play an active role in the treatment process, you will increase the chances of success a hundredfold.

Separation Anxiety

Have you ever left the house, sometimes for only a few minutes, and returned to find that your "best friend" has chewed the furniture, barked, howled, and eliminated on the carpet. If your dog behaves this way when you leave your home, it is probably suffering from the behavior problem known as *separation anxiety*. Before separation anxiety can be treated successfully, it is helpful to know what causes it.

Dogs are considered pack animals; that is, they prefer to run in groups rather than individually. As its owner, you will be considered by the dog to be part of its "pack" and the dog will constantly want to associate with you. When you leave, you separate the dog from its pack, creating separation anxiety. This is especially true for the Vizsla. The behavior is magnified if you make a big fuss over the dog when leaving or returning to the house; furthermore, your dog will associate your behavior patterns, such as rattling the car keys or turning off the television, with your departure.

Treatment. When treating separation anxiety, remember that it is an instinctive behavior; it is not related to disobedience or lack or training. As a result, negative reinforcement for the act tends to be unrewarding; in fact, most of these dogs would rather be punished than left alone. The key to treating this problem lies in planning short-term absences, then gradually lengthening them until your dog gets used to being alone for a while. Begin by stepping out of the house for only a few seconds (10 to 15) at a time for the first few days or so. Your dog will learn that you will return soon. Vary your training session times throughout the day. The idea is to gradually lengthen the time you are away so that your departures soon become routine to the dog.

Points to keep in mind when attempting to break your Vizsla of this annoying behavior are:

1. Don't make a fuss over your dog within 5 to 10 minutes of your arrival at or departure from home. This will help keep the excitement and anxiety levels in your dog to a minimum.

2. During your training sessions, try not to reenter the house while the dog is performing the undesirable act. Doing so will only serve to positively reenforce the dog to repeat the act.

3. Eliminate any behavior that may signal your departure to your Vizsla, such as rattling your car keys or saying "Good-bye" to your dog.

4. For the dog that likes to chew a lot, provide plenty of nylon chew bones to occupy its time while you are gone.

5. Leaving the television or radio on while you're gone seems to keep the dog from feeling lonely and abandoned in some cases.

In severe cases, veterinarians can prescribe antianxiety medications such as amitriptyline HCl to help assist in the treatment of separation anxiety, so don't hesitate to consult your veterinarian if you are having difficulty controlling your dog's separation anxiety problem.

Barking

Let's face it—some Vizslas just love to hear themselves talk. Unfortunately, most owners and their neighbors hardly share the same feeling. There is no doubt that dogs that bark excessively are a nuisance and can cause many a sleepless night. For this reason, correction of the problem is essential to your sanity, and to that of those around you.

A dog may bark excessively for a number of reasons. The first is boredom. Vizslas that have nothing else to do may simply "sing" to themselves to whittle the time away. Another potential cause is territoriality. Outsiders, whether human or animal, will almost always elicit a bark out of a dog if that outsider is threatening to encroach upon its territory. Dogs may also use the bark indiscriminately to warn others to stay away. In such instances, the barking episode may be tipped off by the far-off bay of a neighborhood dog or the slamming of a car door down the street.

Separation anxiety is another common source of nuisance barking. Some dogs have such severe cases that they bark continuously when their owner leaves them, even for a short period of time. Often, the owner will return home to find the dog hoarse from barking.

Treatment. When attempting to break your dog of this annoying habit, always remember this principle: If you respond to your dog's barking by yelling at it or physically punishing it, you are going to make the problem worse. Dogs isolated from their owners for most of the day don't care what kind of attention they receive. It can be positive or negative as long as they get some. Dogs that are barking out of boredom or from separation anxiety will soon learn that their action will eventually get them attention, and they'll keep doing it. Even dogs that are barking for other reasons can catch on quickly that such vocalization will bring them a bonus of attention from their beloved owners. As a result, no matter how angry you get, or how sleepy you are, avoid the urge to punish your dog for its barking.

The first thing you need to determine is whether or not separation anxiety has anything to do with the problem. If you think it does, treat it as you would any other case of separation anxiety (see page 33). In many cases, dogs that bark for this reason alone can be broken of their habit. Keep in mind, though, that the source of the barking may involve a combination of factors, not just one.

Vizslas that bark for reasons other than separation anxiety need to be given more attention throughout the day. A dog that tends to bark through the night should be given plenty of exercise in the evening to encourage a good night's sleep. A nylon chew bone can be helpful in diverting its attention. Feeding its daily ration later in the evening may also promote contentment for the night.

If your dog's barking occurs at a certain time of day or night consider moving it to a different part of the house. If your Vizsla is housed outdoors, bring it inside the house or garage. This, of course, may not be possible if you failed to instruct your dog about the ways of household living when it was a puppy. Nevertheless, removing your dog from its "primary" territory and/or increasing the amount of contact with members of its pack can help curb its urge to bark. Also, if feasible, encourage your neighbors to keep their pets indoors at night, since nighttime roaming of neighborhood dogs and cats are major causes of nuisance barking.

House Soiling

It has happened to all of us: the early morning discovery in the family room, the unexpected (or sometimes expected) surprise awaiting our arrival home from work: house soiling. It is a dirty habit, especially considering the size of the Vizsla. In many of these cases, the problem had an origin traceable to puppyhood; for others, it results from developmental behavioral or health problems. Regardless of the cause, you can take an active role in most cases to minimize or stop completely this annoying habit.

Don't expect to break your dog of this nasty habit by sticking its face and nose in the excrement after the fact. Not only is this action illogical, some dogs may even enjoy it! Instead, you need to take a more rational approach to identifying the cause and solving the problem.

Lack of or improper house-training during puppyhood is undoubtedly the most common cause of house soiling. Many Vizsla owners can't understand why their puppy has no problems eliminating on newspaper, but just can't get the knack of going outside when the newspapers aren't there. They seem to forget that, to a puppy, newspaper and grass are two different surfaces with different

Show respect for your dog's "private property," such as his chew toys.

smells. To paper-train a puppy, and then expect it to switch easily to another type of surface is asking a lot, and often presents a confusing dilemma to the poor little thing. Puppies need to be taught right from the start to go outside to eliminate. At the same time, Vizslas that are going to be kept in an outdoor enclosure still need to be house-trained as puppies, just in case the need later arises to bring them indoors. If you miss this

chance when your Vizsla is a puppy, you'll be in for trouble later on.

Contrary to popular opinion, you *can* teach an old dog new tricks—it just takes longer. With older canines that weren't properly housebroken, proceed with training or retraining as you would a puppy. Along with lots of praise, a favorite treat or snack can also be used to reinforce the desired behavior.When you can't be at home to monitor indoor activity, put the dog in a crate, travel kennel, or small bathroom, since dogs are less likely to have premeditated accidents in such confined spaces. Just be reasonable as to the amount of time you make it wait between eliminations.

Separation anxiety can also cause inappropriate elimination. Dogs left on their own will often become frustrated and soil one or more parts of the house as a result. Some dogs will target furniture, bedding, and, if kept in the garage, even the roofs of automobiles. If the cause is separation anxiety, most of this adverse behavior will occur within 15 to 20 minutes after the owner departs; such predictability can help you in your efforts to correct the problem. Treat the behavior as you would any other case of separation anxiety.

The desire to delineate territory is another reason a dog may choose to urinate or defecate indiscriminately. Certainly, intact males are more prone to this instinctive activity. Dogs have such a keen sense of smell that the mere presence of a canine trespasser around the perimeter of the home can set off a urine-marking binge. Owners who move into previously owned homes often find out the hard way that the former owners had a poorly trained or highly territorial house dog. Unfortunately, in this case neutering your pet may or may not be helpful, depending upon its age. In many older males, it has become more habit than hormonal, and neutering does little to prevent it. Use of a pet odor neutralizer on the carpet and baseboards is warranted if you suspect that a previous occupant is to blame. The use of fencing or dog repellent (*not* poison) around the perimeter of the house may also help keep urine-markers away from your house.

An extremely submissive behavior often results in a cowering dog that urinates whenever anyone approaches. This type of elimination is common in dogs that experienced adverse socialization as puppies or spent most of their growing years in a kennel or pound. Management of such behavior focuses upon your actions and body language when approaching or greeting the dog. Try to avoid direct eye contact and sudden physical contact; by doing so, you can send the dog into immediate submissiveness. If you've been gone from the house for a while, avoid sudden and exuberant greetings when you get home. By ignoring it initially, you'll lower your dog's excitement level, reduce the immediate threat to it, and give it no reason to urinate. One trick you can try is immediately and casually to walk over to your dog's food bowl and place some food or treats in it. The idea is to distract its attention away from the excitement of your arrival, and create a more comfortable, pleasing situation for it. Once you've been home for a while, you can and should offer more of your attention.

Some diseases or illnesses can cause a pet to urinate or defecate indiscriminately; for example, dogs that persistently defecate inside the house should be checked for internal parasites. Increasing the fiber content in your pet's diet can also increase the amount of trips it needs to take outdoors. Certainly if the stools are semiformed, or seem to differ in normal appearance or consistency, an underlying medical reason should be suspected. Some of the conditions that can increase the frequency of urination include urinary tract infections, kidney disease, and diabetes mellitus. For this reason, don't just assume that your dog's soiling problem is purely emotional. Have potential medical causes ruled out first; then you can concentrate on behavior modification.

Cleaning up. Just a word about cleaning up an accident in the house. When using cleaners to tackle the initial mess, be sure they don't contain ammonia. Dog urine contains a form of ammonia, and such products may actually attract your dog back to the same spot later on. Along this same line, after the initial manual cleaning, your next job is to ensure that residual smell doesn't attract your pet back to the same spot. To accomplish this, you need to employ a product containing odor neutralizers specifically targeted for dogs. These products are available in grocery or pet supply stores. Room deodorizers should not be used; it is virtually impossible to completely mask or hide a scent from the keen canine nose—or, indeed, from most human noses.

Digging

Although separation anxiety can cause digging, the cause is usually sheer boredom or instinctive behavior. Dogs with nothing else to do may opt for yard excavation to simply help pass the time or use up extra energy. The urge to break out of confinement and roam the neighborhood can also

Problem digging can have several underlying causes, including sheer boredom.

compel a dog to start digging. Some dogs will dig a hollow in which to lie and stay cool on a hot day. Many dogs like to bury such personal items as bones or toys for exhumation at a later date. Such instinctive behavior, though annoying, can hardly be considered abnormal, and thus is difficult to totally eliminate.

Increasing your dog's daily dose of exercise may be just what the doctor ordered to help relieve its boredom and release any pent-up energy. Diverting the attention of a chronic digger is another plausible treatment approach; for instance, some troublesome cases have responded very well to the addition of another canine playmate. Rawhide bones and other chewing devices can also be used as attention-grabbers, but only if they don't end up underground themselves. If most of the digging occurs at night, overnight confinement to the garage may be the answer to spare your yard from the ravages of your dog's claws. Finally, if not already done, neutering can help snuff out the strong urge to dig in dogs that want to roam.

Destructive Chewing

Many canines are literally "in the doghouse" with their owners because of this destructive behavior. No one wants a pet that seeks and destroys any inanimate object it can sink its teeth into; however, personal property damage is not the only reason to eliminate such behavior. Many of these chewers also end up in veterinary hospitals suffering from gastroenteritis or intestinal obstructions; therefore, such adverse activity can cost more than just replacement value of furniture or fixtures—it can sometimes cost the life of a pet!

In puppies, destructive chewing can easily arise from lack of training and from the inappropriate selection of toys by the owner. Although puppies are naturally going to explore their

34

environment with their mouths, they need to learn at an early age what is and isn't acceptable to chew on. Solid command training is a must in these young pups. Avoid providing such common household items as old shoes, T-shirts, or sweatshirts as toys to play with. Puppies can't tell the difference between an old shoe and a new shoe, and may decide to try out your new pair for a snack one afternoon. Objects that repeatedly bear the brunt of your dog's teeth should be placed as far out of reach as possible. Spray pet repellents around areas that are out of bounds to make a mischievous puppy think twice before sinking its teeth into a sofa leg or chair cushion. To save your pet from a potentially fatal electric shock smear lamp cords with a bitter substance available in pet supply stores.

In young to middle-aged Vizslas, separation anxiety is probably the number one cause of destructive chewing. In these cases, the destructive behavior results from an owner's departure from the house, even for a few minutes. In these instances, correction of the problem should focus upon correction of the anxiety attack (see page 33).

Finally, as with problem barking, boredom leads to destructive chewing in some adult dogs. If you think this may be the case, increase your dog's daily activity, and provide it with plenty of alternative targets, such as rawhides or nylon bones, on which to chew. Divert its attention, and its chewing probably will be diverted as well.

Jumping

When you talk about annoying behavior, this one is right up there with house soiling and incessant barking. "Jumpers," are usually right there at the door when visitors call, and have an innate tendency to spoil a perfectly cordial greeting. After all,

visitors may object when a dog with dirty paws jumps on their nice, clean clothes, especially if the dog weighs 50 pounds (23 kg) or more!

This is one problem behavior that should never be allowed. Probably the best way to assure this is through strict command training, starting at an early age. Until it learns its commands, be sure to discourage the puppy from jumping on you or family members. When it does jump at or on you, quickly push it off with your hands and shout "No." As an alternative, flex your knee and make sudden, but gentle, contact with its chest, pushing it backwards.

For adult dogs that never learned their manners, a refresher course in command training is the most effective method of curing the chronic jumper. Sometimes, dogs that jump may be simply trying to tell their owners that they want more attention. In such cases, a few more moments of your time devoted to your pet each day is an important adjunct to therapy.

Fear of Loud Noises

Fear induced by loud noises such as thunder or gunshots can be a common cause of aberrant behavior in Vizslas. Many people may argue that because of dogs' ultrasensitive hearing, pain caused by the noise may play a bigger role than fear itself. Regardless of the reason, when confronted with the disturbing sound, these dogs can become hysterical and destructive in their attempts to escape, and injure themselves or their owners in the process.

If your dog fears the sound of thunder, fireworks or gunshots, avoid direct attempts at comforting your pet, since doing so would be indirectly rewarding the undesirable behavior. If your dog is the type that becomes unglued in these situations, consider letting it "ride out the storm" in its travel kennel. In addition, loudly play a radio or television in the vicinity of the pup to muffle some of the fearful sounds and make it feel more at ease. Your veterinarian can prescribe antianxiety medications for your dog if it has an exceptional fear of loud noises, but these medications should be used sparingly and only as needed.

Contrary to popular belief, gun nervousness is not an instinctive behavior, but rather a learned one in gundogs. As a result, steadiness in the presence of gunfire must be taught early and correctly. Gun nervousness should be differentiated from actual gun-shyness. If a pup is nervous around a gun, it will act quite startled when the gun is discharged and may be reluctant to respond to your commands. These dogs may also quickly lose their desire for the hunt, wanting instead to remain meekly at the side of their owner. The condition results from an improper introduction to the firearms and the traumatic mental imprint that results.

Gun-shyness, on the other hand, is a rare phenomenon, but when it rears its ugly head, it usually spells disaster. Gun-shyness is an inherited defect characterized by terrified reaction to gunfire that sends the dog off into a panicked flight. Unfortunately, dogs suffering from true gun-shyness rarely make acceptable hunting dogs.

If you suspect that your Vizsla may be truly gun-shy, or if your dog remains nervous around the sound of gunfire even after training, consult your veterinarian. He or she will be able to recommend behavior modification therapies that can be employed in an attempt to salvage your Vizsla's usefulness as a hunter. Although success rates in treating true gun-shyness are fair to poor, it is worth your time to explore such treatment options, considering the alternative.

Purchasing a puppy from a reputable breeder will greatly reduce the chances of acquiring a gun-shy dog. If possible, ask the breeder to demonstrate that the pup is not gun-shy, or test it yourself shortly after purchase. A reputable breeder will take back a dog of his or her breeding for any reason, including gun-shyness. Purchasing a partially trained or fully trained gundog that has been properly introduced to firearms will virtually eliminate this chance altogether.

Aggressiveness

Of the undesirable behaviors a dog may exhibit, this is certainly the most disturbing and is unacceptable. Aggressiveness may be directed toward other dogs or other species, including humans. Certainly, dogs that display aggressiveness to people pose special problems to their owners in terms of liability as well as injury. Fortunately, aggressiveness is a rare problem in the Vizsla.

Dominance certainly plays an important role in canine aggressiveness. Some dogs refuse to submit to authority and will lash out at anyone or anything that attempts to exert that authority. In many instances, these dogs were not properly trained and socialized when they were young; in others, sex hormones, particularly testosterone, may have a strong influence as well.

Treatment for aggressiveness consists of a return to basic command and obedience training. In addition, exercises designed to reestablish dominance can be recommended by your veterinarian and should also be performed. Only experienced dog owners who are physically strong and psychologically assertive should attempt this kind of training. Most dog owners should consider hiring a trainer who specializes in this problem. If the aggressiveness is directed toward a particular person in general, he or she should be included in these exercises. Use extreme caution and a good, strong muzzle before you attempt dominance assertion. For aggressive male dogs, neutering is recommended before retraining.

Fear and pain are also common causes of aggression. If a dog feels threatened or overwhelmingly fearful, it naturally experiences a "fight or flight" syndrome and may choose the former option over the latter. In addition, dogs have been known naturally to lash out in fear or pain at humans or other animals. Sudden aggressive changes in personality with or without signs of illness warrant a complete checkup by your veterinarian.

Treating fear-induced aggression is aimed at reducing the threat you or others pose to your pet. If fear aggression is induced by an outside stimulus, such as a gunshot, then proper restraint and isolation are recommended while the stimulus lasts. If a dog suffers from a vision or hearing deficit, attract the dog's attention before you approach it.

Physical punishment is not only a useless tool for training but also a cause of aggressive backlash because of pain and fear. This is just one more reason why such negative reinforcement should be avoided.

If a dog suffers from injuries or illness, always approach and handle it with caution, for although it may not mean to, it could exhibit aggressive behavior because of pain associated with the ailment.

Territorial aggressiveness toward unwelcome animals or people is not uncommon, as any utilities meter reader would attest to. Dogs—male or female—will certainly defend property they feel is theirs, and may not hesitate to fight for it. Such aggressive behavior can be just as easily sparked by a perceived encroachment while the dog is eating or playing with its favorite toy. Many bite wounds result from such careless actions.

A return to the basics of command training with or without neutering should help curb territorial aggressiveness. Neutering will usually help in most cases.

Showing respect for a dog's eating privacy and "private property" (toys, bowls, and other belongings) is a commonsense way to avoid aggressive behavior. It is of vital importance to impress this on children, since they can be frequent violators of the rule. If a dog seems particularly possessive over toys or bones, eliminate all but one or two of the items. Also, consider feeding the dog in an isolated area of the house away from disturbances.

The best treatment for most types of aggression is prevention. By adhering to the principles of proper socialization and by proper command training, most behavioral problems related to aggressiveness can be avoided altogether; however, for any Vizsla exhibiting aggressiveness, a thorough physical examination and

Daily exercise will keep your Vizsla fit and trim.

Proper training will make it easy for you to exercise your Vizsla.

consultation with a veterinarian is indicated. Ruling out underlying medical causes is certainly one reason for this; the other is that your veterinarian may choose to prescribe medications to assist in retraining efforts or as a direct attempt to curb the psychological aspects of your dog's aggressiveness. Human antianxiety medications such as amitriptyline HCl and diazepam are being used more and more in veterinary medicine as effective replacements for progestin hormonal therapy (which can have many unpleasant side effects) to help assist in the correction of many behavioral problems, including aggressiveness. Ask your veterinarian for more details.

Exercising Your Vizsla

You can tremendously improve your Vizsla's quality of life and performance by incorporating a moderate exercise program into its daily routine. It will improve cardiovascular endurance and function, help tone and tighten muscles, and improve recovery times, allowing your dog to work longer and harder during the hunt or competition. For relatively sedentary Vizslas not used for hunting or competitive events, exercise will help maintain muscle tone and strength. It will also improve your dog's agility and flexibility, and help loosen up those stiff joints. Regular exercise will also promote and improve gastrointestinal motility, stimulating nutrient absorption and ensuring maximum utilization. Finally, exercise will help keep your Vizsla's weight in check, preventing all the health problems that accompany obesity.

Before implementing any exercise program for your Vizsla, a complete physical exam should be performed by your veterinarian to identify any underlying health conditions that may limit the type and amount of exercise. Be sure to follow your veterinarian's advice closely in designing a fitness program around the special needs of your individual pet.

There are several avenues to take in order to heighten and strengthen your Vizsla's condition. Swimming is great exercise and can often be combined with retrieval training. It is especially useful for increasing cardiovascular endurance and toning certain muscle groups. Jogging or walking with your Vizsla is also an excellent way to maintain or improve cardiovascular fitness, not only for your Vizsla but for you as well! Twenty to thirty minutes every other day is a good goal. Because of their size, Vizslas make great jogging partners and can keep up with the best foot racers. Check with your doctor before undertaking such a program yourself!

Be sure to allow a ten-minute warm-down following any strenuous activity. Also, provide your Vizsla access to plenty of fresh water to allow for replacement of fluids lost during physical exertion. Isotonic sport drinks or electrolytic formulas available from your local convenience store or grocery are also effective means of replenishing lost fluids and electrolytes.

Physical Conditioning for Hunting Season

About 60 days before the beginning of hunting season, plan on implementing a conditioning program for both you and your dog to prepare you physically for the big days that lie ahead. As far as your dog's conditioning program is concerned, plan on gradually increasing the number of trips into the field as time permits. Ideally, if you can get your dog into the field three to five times weekly for 45 to 90 minutes at a time, it will undoubtedly be in top condition when hunting season arrives. Beginning a conditioning program early will also allow time for your dog's footpads to toughen in preparation for traveling the rough fields and woods it is likely to encounter in the days to come.

Neutering for Health

The term neutering refers to the removal of the ovaries and uterus (ovariohysterectomy) in the female dog or the testicles (castration) in the male. Because of the high incidence of reproductive disorders in older dogs, it is recommended that all dogs be neutered by their eighth birthday. By having this procedure performed, age-related uterine infections and pyometra in older females can be avoided, and the incidence of prostate disorders in aging males greatly reduced. As an added benefit, if you are not planning on breeding your female, those that have had this procedure performed before their second heat cycle are at a lesser risk of developing mammary cancer at a later age than are their non-neutered counterparts.

Neutering your Vizsla won't lead to laziness and obesity—there are plenty examples of slim and trim neutered dogs running around debunking this myth. Improper feeding practices, lack of exercise, and, in some instances, disease, cause obesity in dogs, not

reproductive status. Furthermore, while it is true that neutering can have a calming effect on nervous or restless Vizslas, activity levels in emotionally stable dogs are rarely affected.

Traveling with Your Vizsla

In all instances involving transport of a dog by car, the safety and comfort of the passenger (and driver, when applicable) must always be kept in mind first and foremost. As a responsible pet owner you can help achieve these goals by following a few basic travel guidelines.

Travel Carriers

To begin, it is always recommended that, when transporting a pet by car, a travel carrier or kennel be used. Not only will your pet feel more secure in a carrier, helping to reduce stress associated with the ride, but it will help minimize jostling and jolting movements that could injure your dog. If your Vizsla is too large to fit comfortably into one of these carriers, then the back seat is the place for the dog. An excited unrestrained pet in the passenger seat of a car creates a dangerous situation. In addition, dogs

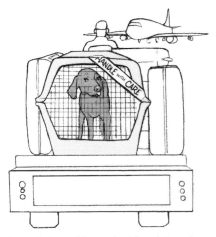

A sturdy kennel is required for air travel.

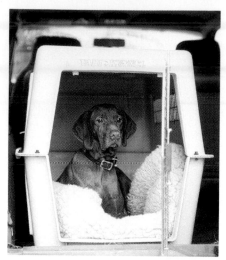

For safety, always use a travel kennel or enclosure when transporting your Vizsla by car.

allowed to ride in front seats can suffer serious or even lethal injuries should airbags deploy in an accident.

Temperature and Air Quality

Be sure to keep the inside of your car well-vented and at a cool temperature. Excited or stressed canines that are forced to travel in hot, stuffy cars or ones filled with cigarette or cigar smoke are likely to suffer ill effects. Cigarette smoke can be irritating to the eyes, nose, and mucous membranes of a dog; therefore, as a courtesy to your canine friend, refrain from smoking until you have reached your final destination. Car exhaust fumes can have the same effect as cigarette smoke, so, if you are stopped in traffic for any appreciable amount of time, be sure to crack the car windows and keep the air in the car circulating continuously.

As you have heard time and time again, *never* leave your dog unattended in a parked car for more than

five minutes on days when environmental temperatures exceed 72°F (22°C) or drop below 55°F (13°C) as heat stroke or hypothermia, respectively, could result. If you have to leave your pet for a few minutes, be sure to leave two or more windows partially open to allow air circulation. In addition, the use of window shields and sun visors or shades is strongly recommended to help keep temperatures in the car at acceptable levels.

Water

For lengthy trips, be sure to take along plenty of water for your dog to drink, and plan on making frequent stops along the way so your Vizsla can relieve itself.

Tip: Consider freezing some water in a bowl before the trip. This "popsicle" can provide a lasting and refreshing source of water for long trips.

If your Vizsla is known to get carsick, try feeding a small amount of food about 30 minutes before your trip; often, an empty stomach coupled with stress can predispose a pet to motion sickness. Never give your dog any medication for anxiety or motion sickness unless it was specifically prescribed by your veterinarian.

Traveling by Plane

Always consult your veterinarian before you transport your Vizsla by plane to determine whether any medical conditions your pet may have could be exacerbated by such a trip; for example, high-altitude flying and temperature and pressure fluctuations could be harmful to a dog that might have an underlying heart disorder. Speak with your airline representatives concerning the airline's accommodations for pets. Variations in policies exist among airline companies; ask your pet health professionals for their recommendations.

Training

Owning a well-trained Vizsla is not only rewarding and fun, but also productive. Proper training allows you to establish your dominance in the relationship between you and your companion right from the start, and can prevent many behavioral problems. Solid training can also keep your friend out of troublesome situations that could threaten both its health and yours.

One characteristic is exhibited by every good trainer: Patience. Without this virtue, you're going to have a hard time teaching your dog anything. You must plan on setting aside time each day for training, and resolve to stick to it. Keep in mind that it will be only a temporary part of your time budget. After all, the more time you devote from the start, the quicker and more satisfying the results.

What about obedience training schools? Are they worth the time and the money? The answer is "yes" if it will motivate you to devote the time for the task at hand; however, for maximum results, you should be physically present during the actual training if at all possible. If desired, enroll in an active participation class in which an instructor directs you and your dog through the training session. Such a class doesn't relieve you of your homework duties, however; you need to practice with your dog daily on your home turf.

The Basics

The magic success formula for all training endeavors is derived from two key concepts: consistency and repetition. Consistency provides the building blocks; repetition is the mortar that holds the program together. Without the two, you may as well try to teach a rock to heel—the results will be the same.

Consistency means more than simply using the same commands over and over again; it also means using the same praises and corrections each time, and keeping your voice tones and whistle commands consistently unique for each. Even your body language and postures during training should remain uniform between sessions. As trivial as it may seem, your Vizsla will pick up on things like that. Dogs like routine, so stick to it. Train at the same hour each day, and for the same length of time for each daily session.

Just as important as consistency to a dog's learning process is repetition.

Be sure to praise heartily when your Vizsla performs as desired.

Repeating an action or training drill over and over will help reinforce the positive response you are looking for; furthermore, the more repetition you implement into training, the more refined your dog's learned skills become.

Use verbal praise instead of physical pain in your training sessions. Dogs, especially puppies, should always be rewarded for a job well done with lots of praise and attention. Food treats are fine as a reward supplement, but never use them to replace verbal compliments.

Negative Reinforcement

Negative reinforcement may be indicated if your puppy or dog purposely disobeys a command or commits an undesirable act; yet this should *never* take the form of physical negative reinforcement. There are alternative means, each of which is just as, if not more, effective than physical reinforcement. Dogs can be reprimanded effectively with a sharp verbal "No." Air horns, a can full of coins, hand-held vacuums, and so on, can all be used to create abrupt noises to quickly gain your dog's attention without inflicting any pain. Aiming a water sprayer at an unruly student is also an effective reinforcement method.

Institute the negative reinforcement quickly, preferably within five seconds of the act. If you don't apply it before this time expires, any later negative reinforcement may satisfy your anger, but will serve no useful training purpose. Don't extend your punishment past a few seconds. Prolonged exhortations will only confuse your pet and cause you to lose your voice.

Avoid using your dog's name during the negative reinforcement. If you do, it may start to associate the name with the bad act and eventually become a nervous wreck whenever its name is called. Reserve this name-calling for positive, happy experiences only.

If you do punish, always follow it with a command or drill that will lead to a praise situation. Always end your time together on a positive note, and you'll make progress in leaps and bounds.

Remember: The most effective training programs rely more on praise than they do on negative reinforcement. For Vizslas, simply withholding praise from them is negative reinforcement enough to modify their behavior. By rewarding your dog for doing something well as opposed to punishing it for doing something bad, you'll get the positive results you are looking for much faster.

Family Members

If possible, involve all members of the family in the training process. An all-too-common scenario is one in which a dog ignores the commands of anyone but the one person who trained it. To avoid this, get the whole family involved, but be sure to remain consistent within the family regarding training methods and commands. Also, only one or two people should be present during a training session; too many "cooks" will only distract your dog.

Verbal Commands

All verbal commands should be kept short and sweet, and using slightly different voice tones for each command will help to prevent confusion. If verbal punishment is to be used, make certain that it is totally different in tone and in presentation than the other commands.

Length of Sessions

Keep initial training sessions short and to the point. For puppies 8 to 12 weeks old, devoting 15 minutes two to three times daily will yield excellent results. As your dog matures, the length of each of these sessions can increase. Let your dog's attitude be your guideline. If it seems bored, indifferent, or has become totally unruly, you have probably exceeded its attention span.

Always end your training session on a good note. Doing so is constructive in terms of your dog's mental development, and effectively sets the tone for the next session.

Establishing Dominance

One of the purposes of training a dog is to establish your dominance in the relationship right from the start. Your dog needs to realize who's boss, who's the head of the pack. This is rarely a problem with Vizslas, as they are eager to please their owners. Even so, there are four effective ways to assert this dominance during your training sessions:

1. *Maintain control of your dog's neck region.* This is especially important in the early stages of training. The collar and leash were originally developed with this principle in mind. Dogs are naturally protective of their neck regions, since, in a fight, this is often the first area that the opponent will attack, which is why most dogs will lower their heads in a menacing gesture if they feel threatened. Puppies grasped by the scruff of the neck by their mother become limp in submission. Along these same lines, when your Vizsla allows you to put a collar on it and maneuver it with leash pressure applied to the neck region, it is submitting itself to your dominant position.

2. *Apply pressure along the back region.* As you will see, this concept comes in handy when teaching your dog to sit or lie down. In nature, one dog will assert its dominance over another by mounting the other's back with its forelegs. By applying direct pressure on the back (such as when teaching to sit) or by simply petting your dog along the neck and back region, you are essentially doing the same.

3. *Always stay calm and relaxed during training sessions.* Dogs can sense their owner's nervousness or distress. Overbearing and stubborn Vizslas (fortunately, they are rare) may try to take advantage of such a situation and refuse to submit to authority. Show an air of confidence and control around your dog and it will catch on quickly that you mean business.

4. *Avoid physical or painful negative reinforcements.* As mentioned before, such outbursts serve no purpose, and could emotionally so upset your Vizsla as to completely ruin a training session. Your dog will be more worried about when the next punishment is coming than learning the training material.

5. *Establish direct eye contact with your Vizsla when giving a command.* Don't be the first to look away; the one who wins the staredown wins the dominance play.

Caution: An overly aggressive dog may refuse to submit, and may see your eye contact as a direct challenge. For these, it's best to avoid the confrontation.

Training Equipment

Equipment you will need for obedience training your Vizsla includes a chain training collar, a 6-foot (1.8 m) leather or web lead, a 32-foot (9.75 m) retractable lead (or nylon check cord), two whistles, and a travel kennel. In addition, for advanced field training, you'll need a .22 caliber blank pistol, a retrieving lure, live game, and

Training Equipment
- Chain training collar (choke collar)
- 32-foot (9.75 m) retractable lead/check cord
- Training whistles
- Travel kennel
- .22 caliber blank pistol
- Retrieving lure
- Release cages
- Live game

The proper fitting of a "choke" collar for a dog being led on the handler's left side.

release cages. Your local hunting and gun clubs can help direct you to sources of the last two items.

Collar. A chain training collar, commonly referred to as a choke collar, is an invaluable training tool. This collar does not actually choke a dog when properly applied, but, rather, is designed to exert quick and temporary pressure on the dog's neck, promoting submission. When applied, the collar should be large enough so that you can comfortably fit two fingers between the collar and the neck with minimal pressure felt on the fingers. For maximum effectiveness and safety, this type of collar should be worn only during training sessions.

Just a quick word about electronic training collars, or "shock" collars. These devices are generally not required for training Vizslas if proper obedience commands are taught at an early age; however, for the unruly student or one that is slow to respond to obedience or field training, electronic training devices may be useful. Be sure to follow the instructions that come with the unit carefully or, better

yet, consult your veterinarian on the proper use of these devices.

Leads. The 6-foot leather lead will come in handy for teaching basic obedience commands, and the 32-foot retractable lead or check cord for controlling range during field training. Leads can be purchased at any pet supply store or discount store. They are also available through mail-order catalogs.

Whistle. Another item you'll want to put on your shopping list is a training whistle. Consider using a whistle instead of your voice to train your dog; it allows for consistent commands every time (not to mention that it will save your voice). Just remember to always carry a spare with you to the field in case your primary whistle malfunctions or you misplaced it. The type of whistle you use is simply a matter of personal preference, but avoid using silent whistles. Also, if you ever have to replace a whistle, make certain the new whistle you purchase is similar in sound and pitch to the one you use to initially train your dog.

Kennel. You will need a travel kennel to transport your dog to and from the field. Be sure the one you get is large enough for your Vizsla to turn around in, yet small enough to prevent unnecessary movement during transport.

Pistol and retrieving lure. Two other pieces of equipment you'll want to purchase if you are planning to use your Vizsla for hunting include a .22 caliber blank pistol and a retrieving lure. You will need the .22 caliber pistol to begin conditioning your pup to the sound of gunfire. These pistols are relatively inexpensive and can be obtained through gun shops, sporting goods stores, and even mail-order catalogs. Also, if you are going to teach your Vizsla to retrieve, you'll need a retrieving lure. These can be obtained commercially or you can make one yourself with a sock, duck tape, and some feathers from an upland game bird, which the texture and firmness of the lure should resemble. A lure that is too hard and solid may promote rough handling ("hard mouth") by your dog, as it must grip it tightly in order to hold on to it.

Obedience Training

Obedience training, which should be started when your puppy is as young as 8 weeks, involves the teaching and practice of basic commands that will allow you to control your dog in any given setting. To achieve maximum training results when obedience training, plan on devoting at least 15 minutes twice a day to the task. Schedule one of these training times immediately upon arrival home from work. Your dog will be excited to have you home and will link the training experience to this pleasure of being reunited with its "pack." Another good time to train is very early in the morning. Puppies are very receptive to learning during this time and a good vigorous training session before you leave for work can help calm dogs that might get anxious at seeing you leave.

The essential obedience commands you will want to teach your Vizsla include *whoa, release, come-in, heel, sit, down, and kennel.* Other specialized commands exist, but these seven are the most useful at home and in the field. Vizslas are intelligent and most puppies will pick up these commands easily.

Whoa

The most important obedience command your Vizsla needs to learn is the command to stop, or whoa. This command tells your dog to stop immediately and stand at attention. In the field, the whoa command will be used to control your dog's range and to keep it staunch when it goes on point. Whoa is also useful for keeping a dog steady to wing and shot, and for reinforcing a dog that is honoring the point

Flexible leads are excellent training tools.

Vizslas are quick to learn and eager to please.

Teaching the stay or whoa command.

of another. Finally, it is an indispensable tool for keeping your dog out of harm's way both at home and while hunting. In fact, never let your puppy run free of its leash or a check cord until this command is fully mastered.

Begin teaching this command by taking your pup for a walk with a flexible lead attached to its chain training collar. As it begins to distance itself from you on the extended lead, get its attention with a "whoa," followed by one long blast on the whistle and a firm tug or jerk on the lead. If it stops, walk up to it slowly, repeating the command "whoa" as you approach. Readjust its position if you see fit to do so, then praise it profusely for a job well done. If your dog doesn't stop on the initial command or if it begins to move when you approach it, repeat the whistle blast, verbal command, and sharp tug on the lead until it complies with your wishes.

Once your dog is stationary, start to walk away slowly, extending the flexible lead by hand. If the dog moves, immediately command it to whoa and walk back to it, repeating the command and praising it if it responds to it. Gradually increase the distance you walk away from your dog with each successive training session until you've finally reached the maximum distance on the leash. Only when you feel your Vizsla has mastered this command should you remove the leash from its collar. Even then, do so within the confines of a restricted area such as a fenced yard, just in case your ambitious pup has a sudden lapse of memory.

Note: If you are training your Vizsla for obedience showing, the command "Stay" is often substituted for "Whoa."

Release

"Release" is a go-ahead command for your dog to begin or resume its activities. With your puppy on its check cord, command it to whoa, immediately followed by one long blast on the whistle. Allow your Vizsla to remain in this standing position for 20 to 30 seconds, then say "Release," immediately followed by two short blasts on your whistle. After giving the command, enthusiastically begin to walk forward and encourage your puppy to follow you with a firm forward

The release command.

tug on the leash. Avoid the desire to say "Come" or "Heel" to your puppy if it fails to move. Instead, simply walk back to it, repeat the command sequence and guide it forward with your hand on its rump if necessary.

Come-In

Begin teaching your Vizsla to come to you by first stopping it using the whoa command. Now walk 10 feet (3 m) away from your dog, again manually extending the flexible lead or check cord as you go. Turn and face your dog, kneel down, and say "Come," followed by three short blasts on your whistle. Most puppies won't hesitate to rush into their trainer's arms. When yours does, heap on the praise. If it is reluctant to come to you, gently apply pressure toward you with its lead, repeating the command as you do.

One word of caution: Never use this command to call in your dog for negative reinforcement; it will only serve to confuse the pup and may actually hinder other training efforts as well.

Heel

An important command you will teach your Vizsla is to heel (walk at your side). To begin, position yourself with your dog's shoulder even with your knee (if training for obedience showing, the dog should be positioned on the handler's left side). Now, in simultaneous fashion, give a quick forward tug on the lead, say "Heel," and start forward. As your dog follows, keep its head level and in control using the leash. Start out by going 5 yards (4.5 m) at a time, then stopping (use your whoa command) to praise for a job well done.

If your dog refuses to move on your initial command, go back to the starting line and set up again. This time, if needed, follow the quick tug with an encouraging push forward from the

Teaching a Vizsla to come-in.

rear end to initiate movement. Start and stop frequently, praising as you go. As your dog starts to catch on, increase the distances you go each time. The ultimate goal is to have it walk briskly by your side until a command is given to do otherwise. If it gets too far out in front of you, a sharp, backward tug on the lead should be used to correct the discrepancy. For those trainees more interested in playing than learning, stop the training session temporarily and ignore or confine your trainee until it settles down. Don't scold it or show any other acknowledgment of its antics. It will soon learn that you mean business.

Once your dog has become comfortable walking in straight lines by your side, take it through some turns to both the right and to the left. During the turns, your dog's shoulder should remain aligned with your knee.

Walking at heel.

The sit command.

Sit and Down

Sit and down are two commands you'll want your dog to learn if it is to compete in obedience trials and dog shows. For the hunter, these two commands are not as vital, yet it certainly won't hurt your dog to learn them.

To teach your Vizsla to sit, start with the whoa command to stop your student. Next, pull upwards on your dog's lead, say "Sit," and push down on its rear just above the tail to encourage it to sit. Have your dog maintain this posture for a good five seconds, then break into a *heel*. Gradually increase the amount of time it stays in the sitting position as your training progresses.

The down command can be taught after your dog has mastered the sit command. Have your dog assume the sitting position, then say "down" while applying downward pressure with your free hand to your dog's shoulder region. Note the difference from the sit command, in which downward pres-

sure is applied to the hind end. Once your dog has assumed the correct position, command it to whoa and begin to slowly walk away. If your dog begins to break position, say "Whoa" once more; if necessary, walk back to your dog and place it again in the *down* position. Repeat the drill over several training sessions until your dog exhibits a consistent satisfactory response.

Kennel

When you say "Kennel" to your dog, it should immediately head for its travel carrier or dog house. To teach your dog this command, attach the retractable lead to its collar, then position the dog approximately 10 feet (3 m) away from its travel carrier, and use the whoa command. Now, saying "Whoa" to keep your dog in place, walk over to the carrier, open the gate, and with your arm pointing toward the entrance, use the command "Kennel." If your Vizsla doesn't move, simply use the lead to reel it in to you and direct it into the kennel. Once your dog goes into the kennel, close the gate behind it and dole out the praise or offer a treat. To gain maximum benefit from the word association, allow your Vizsla to remain inside the kennel for a good two minutes before releasing. Keep repeating this process until the desired results are achieved without further physical intervention on your part.

If you are not planning to use your Vizsla for hunting or competition, obedience training is all it will need; however, if you want to have a hunter, field training will be needed as well to mold and enhance certain behaviors and hunting patterns in your dog.

Field Training

Between the ages of 2 and 4 months, your puppy should be introduced to the field. Between 4 and 9 months, its pointing and retrieving abilities should be refined and firearm conditioning begun. Finally, between 9 and 14 months, advanced field training techniques, such as honoring another dog's point and remaining steady to wing and shot, can be taught. Your ultimate goal is to have a trained dog in the field soon after its first birthday. Don't make the mistake of expecting perfection from your dog during its first few seasons; instead, the hands-on experience will serve as training to refine your dog's skills. Perfection will come with practice, and patience and diligence on your part will be rewarded.

Ideally, field training sessions should be held at least twice a week. For Vizsla puppies under 4 months, hold your training to a maximum of 20 minutes per session. Every week or so add five minutes to the training session, working up to a maximum of 60 minutes for dogs under 8 months old. Also, space out your training

sessions as evenly as possible during the week; for instance, holding one session on a Wednesday and the other on a Saturday or Sunday is better than holding both sessions on a weekend.

Finding a field in which to run your pup can be challenging, especially if you live in a city or a suburb; however, there are certain sources to which you can look to find open space in order to train your Vizsla. The first resources to tap are friends and family who own land or may be able to refer you to landowners who live close by. Don't be afraid to hop in a car and drive 30 miles (49 km) to find a field. The investment in time and gas will pay off in dividends during hunting season. Another way to find a field is to approach local landowners directly. You'll be surprised—most will be more than happy to honor your request, especially if you offer to pay a small fee for the privilege of using their land. You can also contact your state's fish and wildlife agency for locations of public lands available for such training purposes. Be sure to state your purpose clearly to them, as many public areas prohibit dogs on the premises. Also, inquire at local dog clubs, hunting clubs, and shooting preserves

Commanding a Vizsla to "kennel."

concerning leased land that is available to members. Joining such a hunting organization will not only allow you to gain access to fields containing game, but will also allow you to network with fellow hunters and other owners of Vizslas. Finally, contact your local sporting goods outlets and gun shops for leads and locations of potential training sites.

Once you've found a field for your Vizsla puppy, introduce the young hunter to it by allowing it to run free and chase any game that it may encounter. The purpose for doing so is to stimulate and develop its instinctive hunting behaviors, including finding and pointing game. Whenever your Vizsla goes on point or performs any desirable action, be sure to praise it profusely for doing so, and it will link the pleasure to the act.

Firearm Conditioning

When your puppy is 4 to 6 months old, you should begin conditioning it to the sound of gunfire. One effective way to get your Vizsla pup used to firearms is to take your .22 caliber blank pistol with you to the field. Let your dog range 20 to 30 yards (18–27 m) ahead of you, position the pistol behind your back, and fire a shot, not-

Teaching a Vizsla to remain staunch on point.

ing your dog's reaction. More than likely the sound will startle it and cause it to look back in your direction. Act as though nothing has happened and soon your eager hunter will forget about it and move on. Repeat the action again 15 minutes later, and continue to do so at frequent intervals throughout the day. During subsequent sessions, gradually decrease the distance between you and your dog before you discharge the pistol. Eventually, after seven to ten training sessions, you should be able to fire the pistol within 5 feet (1.5 m) of your dog without causing alarm.

Once your Vizsla becomes accustomed to the sound of a .22 caliber blank pistol, graduate to a shotgun. Check with local authorities to determine whether shooting is allowed in the area. As with the initial training, begin at a distance, then gradually decrease the range between you and your dog over subsequent training sessions. When firing the shotgun in the dog's presence, aim high in the air and shoot in the direction of the dog. Again, if your dog appears startled, act as though nothing has happened. By repeating this procedure over several weeks, your dog should not even bat an eye when a gun is discharged.

Firearm training can also be combined with retrieval training. Have a partner entice your dog with a lure, then throw it high into the air in front of your dog. When your dog's attention turns to the lure, discharge your gun. Again, if your dog stops and stares back at you, act as though nothing has happened— its attention will soon go back to the lure. With continued conditioning, your dog will learn to relate the sound of gunfire as a "get-ready" signal to retrieve.

One final note: To further solidify your dog's acceptance of gunfire, plan on hunting solo during your dog's first season, and try to limit your shots at game to one each. Rookie dogs that are led out into the field and exposed to a barrage of gunfire from a group of overzealous hunters can easily become startled and refuse to hunt.

Staunchness on Point

Pointing out game is a strong natural instinct in your Vizsla, but remaining staunch on that point may not be. Remaining staunch on point means that your dog will hold a tight point until released by you. Teaching a dog to remain staunch on point greatly increases the pleasure of the hunting experience, affording you greater control and giving you time to walk up on the identified game and position yourself for the shot before it is flushed.

There are three types of points that your Vizsla will exhibit:

1. The first is called a *productive point.* This is a point in which game has been located and is being held by your dog. Certainly, in these cases, staunchness is very important.

2. The second type of point is an *unproductive point,* in which residual scents left by game that has recently left the area are so strong that the dog is fooled into thinking that the game is still there.

3. The third and final type of point is the *false point,* usually caused by a weak air scent or an old, diluted foot scent. As your dog is moving back and forth through a field or woods it may detect this faint scent and stop for a moment and appear to be on point. In most instances, such encounters do not result in a staunch point, as the dog soon realizes what has happened and continues the hunt.

To teach your Vizsla to remain staunch on point, you'll need live game. The most popular types of birds used for this type of training are either pigeons or quail. These birds can be placed in small release cages that can be manually or electronically opened to release the game as desired.

To begin this training, strategically place your release cages containing the birds in a field or wooded area (Vizslas are smart; be sure your dog isn't watching you do this). Next, keeping your dog on its retractable lead or check cord, face it into the wind and slowly approach the release cages. As your dog nears the cages, it will pick up the scent of the birds and should instinctively go on point. When it does, say "Whoa," grab its collar to keep it in position, and praise it. Still maintaining a grip on the collar, adjust your dog's conformation as needed. Tighten the point by pushing your dog's rear end gently in the direction of the bird. As you do, it will instinctively plant its feet firmly and tighten its conformation. If your dog begins to break point, shout "Whoa" and return it to its position. Repeat this process over several training sessions until you are satisfied with your dog's ability to staunchly hold a point.

Steadiness to Wing and Shot

Dogs that are taught to remain steady to wing and shot will maintain their station even after the game is flushed, moving only when released

Steadiness to wing and shot is a characteristic of a well-trained hunting dog.

Diligent training will produce a highly polished and refined gundog.

by the hunter to retrieve the game or to resume hunting. Teaching your dog this skill will prevent it from blindly running after game and flushing out other birds in the process. You'll have greater control over your hunting companion and the productivity of your hunt will increase. Many experts believe that steadiness to wing and shot is the sign of only the most highly polished and trained gundogs.

To teach steadiness, lead your dog through the same process as described for teaching staunchness on point, but this time you'll want to release the birds from their cages or have an assistant throw one of the birds into the air once your dog has tightened its point. Be sure you have a firm grip on your dog's collar and use the command "Whoa" when the birds are flushed. If your dog attempts to break point, command "Whoa" again and tug it back in place. Be patient with your Vizsla, as this is an exciting

time for it. Repeat this process through several training sessions, removing the lead or check cord as your dog becomes more proficient. Soon, you'll have a hunter that won't budge even when tempted by game on the wing.

To teach steadiness to shot, repeat the above sequence, but this time fire your .22 caliber blank pistol when the birds take to flight. If your Vizsla breaks point, use the check cord and the whoa command to return it to position. As your pointer becomes proficient over time, graduate to a shotgun. Repeat the training sequence over and over until you are able to remove the lead or check cord with the assurance that your dog won't bolt when you fire.

Retrieval Training

Retrieving fallen game is natural for many Vizslas; but remember, this is not the breed's primary instinct. There are three types of retrievals you can ask your dog to perform. The first is

Retrieval training.   *A well-trained hunting dog remains steady on point.*

retrieving birds shot off a point. The second is retrieving game shot down in what is called a "hunt dead." This type of retrieve occurs when a dog is brought into a defined area in order to scent and find fallen game that could not otherwise be located. The third type of retrieve, called nonslip retrieving, is for hunting waterfowl and dove. Here, your dog remains at your heel or in your blind until game is shot, then is sent to retrieve it either on land or in water.

One aspect of retrieval training is to teach your dog to have a "soft mouth," that is, to retrieve game tenderly to your hand. It does no good to have your Vizsla retrieve game if it returns a mutilated bird to you. Keep in mind that it is instinctive for dogs to roughly handle game that is wounded and struggling. As a result, use a lure as opposed to live game during retrieval training to prevent this instinctive reaction. Be sure to teach and praise your

dog for a soft mouth early in its life and never play tug-of-war with your Vizsla pup. Although this may seem part of the fun of puppyhood, it only encourages a "hard-mouthed" hunter.

Training your dog to retrieve properly involves more than just throwing a lure off into the distance and having your dog go fetch it. For maximum results, this exercise should be performed in the field with an assistant and a gun. To start, command your Vizsla to heel at your side and attach a lead or check cord to its collar. Next, have your assistant, who is standing next to you, throw the lure high in the air 10 yards (9 m) out in front . When the lure is released, fire your gun into the air. Wait at least 10 seconds after the lure has hit the ground, then give the *retrieve* command and motion to the fallen game. If necessary, lead your dog to the fallen lure and place it in its mouth. Command your dog to whoa and walk back to your original position.

Honoring another dog's point.

Once your Vizsla has the lure in its mouth, command it to *come-in* verbally or with three short blasts on the whistle. If it does not respond immediately, give a firm tug on the check cord to remind it who is in control. When your dog gets within 10 feet (3 m) of you, command it to heel at your side. Reach down and remove the lure from its mouth and praise for a job well done. If your student is overly rough with the lure, or won't let go of it, give a verbal reprimand and manually open its mouth to release the lure.

As with teaching other commands, repeat the process again and again over several training sessions until your dog has mastered it.

Honoring a Point

You must teach your Vizsla to honor another hunting dog's point if you plan on going to the field with fellow hunters whose own dogs are hunting with them. When a dog honors another's point, it refrains from rushing in to supplant the dog that originally located and pointed the game. It is the ultimate in hunting dog etiquette.

To train your dog to honor another's point, you'll obviously need a friend with an experienced gundog to assist in the training. To begin, plant a release cage containing a game bird in a field or wooded area and let the other experienced dog find the bird and go on point. Next, with your dog on a lead, bring it up to within 10 feet (3 m) of the other dog. As your dog nears, it should instinctively go on point. If it doesn't, use the whoa command to stop it. Have your friend release the bird from its cage. Keep your dog steady with a firm grip on its collar and don't allow it to break. Talk to your dog gently, reinforcing with the whoa command if necessary. Release your Vizsla only after the other dog has been released. By repeating this sequence enough times, your dog will soon learn that oft-quoted rule of life—"finder's keepers."

Nutritional Guidelines for Optimum Health

Proper nutrition is the cornerstone of an active, healthy life for your dog, and good nutritional management has a profound positive impact on the Vizsla's performance in the field. Fortunately, as the amount of research supporting the link between diet and health increases, so does the quality of foods available for your pet.

Hundreds of years ago, the diet of most domesticated dogs consisted primarily of table scraps, supplemented by whatever other consumables or prey they could uncover while roaming within the confines of their man-made territories. Today, the commercial dog food industry exceeds $100 million a year in the United States alone, with literally hundreds of products and brand names available for the choosing. As a result, your mission as a prudent dog owner is to choose the food for your Vizsla that is most nutritionally complete and balanced for the dog's stage of life and activity level. Many breeders and trainers advocate the formulation of food at home, using meat and other natural ingredients as raw materials. While such food can provide excellent nutrition, it is vital that they be prepared properly and contain a balance of nutrients that can be used readily by the dog. Dog food companies invest millions of dollars in research developing their premium foods, ensuring that they are of superior nutritional quality. The bottom line: Unless you simply enjoy putting in the time and effort preparing your pet's meal, feeding a home-made diet affords no advantages over feeding a high-quality, premium commercial diet.

Puppies

For Vizslas, puppyhood begins at birth and lasts for approximately 14 months. During this stage of life, your puppy will need to take in appropriate levels of calcium and phosphorus, protein, vitamins, and energy (calories) to ensure proper growth. To be sure your puppy receives the nutrition it needs for correct development, it should be fed a high-quality, nutritionally balanced premium puppy food. Shop for quality, not price, when selecting food for your pup. Since there are so many to choose from commercially, ask your veterinarian which one he or she recommends. Remember that the first year of your puppy's life sets the stage for the degree of health and happiness in later years. As a result, investing in good nutrition during this crucial stage of life is vital.

When feeding high-quality, premium diets to your puppy, vitamin and mineral supplementation is generally not required. Feed the manufacturer's recommended daily amount for the size and weight of your pup. Divide the daily allowance into two feedings, one in the morning and one in the evening. Leave the food down for 20 minutes, allowing your pup to eat all it wants in that time, then remove the food entirely until the next meal. Your puppy will quickly learn to eat on schedule if it expects to be satisfied.

Dogs engaged in vigorous physical activity require a boost in nutrition.

The nutritional needs of your Vizsla will change as it matures.

Avoid giving table food, table scraps, or treats and snacks to your puppy, as this will upset the balance of its daily nutrition.

Keep plenty of clean, fresh water accessible at all times for your pet. Filtered water is recommended for canines for the same reasons it is recommended for humans. Be sure to change the water daily and thoroughly clean the water bowl at least once a week.

Don't encourage begging.

Mature Dogs

At 12 months, plan on switching your dog over to a maintenance-type diet for adults. If possible, use the same brand of food (same manufacturer) to ensure that the transition to the adult ration is smooth. Be aware that so-called maintenance foods that make the claim "complete and balanced for all life stages" are actually puppy foods, since they have been formulated to meet the needs of the most demanding life stage—growth. As a result, they contain an excess of nutrients for the adult dog. Just as researchers have found that the excessive intake of certain dietary nutrients, such as phosphorus, sodium, and fat, are harmful for humans over long periods, certain excesses may also contribute to such health problems as kidney failure, heart failure, obesity, and diabetes in dogs as they grow older. Also, we know that reducing the level of key nutrients in the adult's diet to meet but not greatly exceed its needs is never harmful. Good-quality, scientifically designed adult maintenance diets always contain these reduced and balanced nutrient levels, and are the diets of choice.

How Often and How Much to Feed.

Most adult dogs can be fed just once a day. As far as amounts are concerned, use the manufacturer's recommended daily feeding amounts, then make some adjustments according to your dog's individual needs and activity levels. For instance, daily caloric needs will generally need to be increased 35 to 40 percent during field training and during hunting season, compared to other times of the year. Also, some dogs will gain weight as they grow older despite eating a recommended daily amount of an adult maintenance diet. Further reducing the portion size for these pets usually results in an unhappy, hungry dog that whines, begs, raids garbage and otherwise protests the unpleasant side effects of a weight-reducing diet. Instead, if you find that your Vizsla has put on a few extra pounds around its midsection, it should be placed on a medically supervised weight-loss program, consisting of increased exercise and a reduced-calorie ration, which is designed to satisfy your pet's hunger without the calories.

Treats

As far as treats for your Vizsla are concerned, they are best reserved for training sessions, but understanding that even the strongest willpower can be shattered in an instance by a pair of forlorn, begging eyes, feel free to keep some kibbles of your dog's regular food handy and offer them as treats between full meals. In addition, strange as it may sound, fresh vegetables cut into bite-size pieces make excellent, low-calorie treats as well. You'd be surprised how many dogs just love to munch on vegetables.

Remember: Dogs naturally don't need dietary variations to satisfy cravings; however, they can learn to crave certain items and become finicky eaters if constantly offered items other than those mentioned.

Bones

Do not offer bones of any kind to your Vizsla, as they can shatter, splinter, or become lodged in the mouth, throat, and gastrointestinal tract. Bones can also lead to nutritional imbalances by adding unwanted amounts of minerals to the diet. Even rawhide bones can pose a threat to an overzealous Vizsla that doesn't like to chew its food, as large pieces of slowly digested rawhide can cause gastrointestinal upset, and, in severe instances, intestinal blockages. Instead, stick with flavored nylon chew bones. These are available at any pet supply store and are good substitutes for real bones and

Keep fresh water available at all times for your Vizsla.

rawhide. Most important, nylon bones are easily digested if consumed, even in large chunks.

Water

As with puppies, fresh water (preferably filtered) should be made available at all times for your adult dog. Be sure to change its water daily and thoroughly clean the water bowl at least once a week.

Senior Adults

Once your Vizsla reaches seven years, dietary changes are warranted to accommodate the effects of aging and the wear and tear on the organ systems of its body. The goal of this senior nutritional program is to provide the highest level of nutrition possible, while at the same time maintaining an ideal body weight, slowing the progression of disease and age-related changes, and reducing or eliminating the clinical manifestations of specific disease conditions. For instance, as your dog's metabolic rate slows and the tendency toward obesity grows with advancing age, increasing the amount of fiber and reducing the amount of fat in the diet can help keep the caloric intake where it needs to be to keep body weight constant. In addition, as the kidneys begin to lose their ability to handle the waste materials that must be removed from the body, dietary adjustments can play a major role in reducing the amounts of waste products the kidneys have to process. Simply reducing the sodium content of a diet can have a significant effect on reducing the workload placed on an aging heart. Finally, since older pets tend to have reduced sensory output (taste and smell), increasing the palatability of a diet can keep even the most finicky senior satisfied. This can be accomplished by warming the food before feeding, mixing a small amount of warm water with the dry food, or

adding flavor enhancers recommended by your veterinarian.

Older dogs suffering from diseased teeth and gums will often go off their feed due to the pain associated with chewing. Also, dogs experiencing a diminished sense of smell because of some type of nasal impediment can also become picky eaters. Needless to say, if you ever notice your dog's food intake decrease over a week, consult your veterinarian. A checkup may be in order just to be on the safe side to be sure that the loss of appetite is not the result of a serious underlying medical disorder.

For healthy, older dogs, a high-quality diet formulated for "senior" or "older" dogs is indicated. These foods typically contain more fiber and less fat to make up for a slowing metabolism associated with age. Increases in fiber content also serve to promote healthy bowel function in older pets. Again, stick with the same brand of food you have been feeding over the years in order to help prevent digestive upset when the transition occurs.

When Your Dog Is Ill

If your Vizsla is suffering from a specific illness, a special diet available from your veterinarian is required; for example, dogs suffering from constipation, certain types of colitis, and diabetes mellitus often require a fiber content in their ration even greater than that found in standard senior formulas. In addition, those older dogs suffering from chronic diarrhea, excessive gas production, or pancreatic problems can often benefit from special diets formulated to be more easily digestible than standard maintenance diets. Recommended dietary management of dogs suffering from heart or kidney disease includes diets that are low in sodium and restricted in protein.

Remember: Because all these prescribed diets are so specialized, be sure to follow your veterinarian's directions regarding amounts and frequency of feedings.

Food and Water Bowls

Be sure both food and water bowls are easily accessible to older dogs. Poor eyesight and arthritic joints can sometimes make it difficult to reach or find the water bowl. Keep fresh, clean water available at all times.

Remember: Dogs suffering from kidney problems or endocrine diseases such as diabetes may drink (and require) excessive amounts of water, so you should refill the water dish several times a day.

Trainees, Hunters, and Competitors

Vizslas that are being trained in the field, hunted, or competed extensively require extra nutrition to fuel the energy expenditures needed for these activities. As a rule, working dogs will require a caloric increase of 35 to 40 percent over the amount required by the more sedentary canine. These dogs will need to extract more energy from their diet; as a result, foods for this purpose must be nutritionally dense and highly digestible. Foods with high-energy density contain higher amounts of fat, which provides more calories per gram than do proteins or carbohydrates. Highly digestible foods refer to rations that can be consumed in smaller

amounts, compared to foods that are less digestible, while still meeting the dog's energy needs. Whenever feeding a highly dense and digestible diet, be sure your dog has access to plenty of water at all times. One big advantage of feeding this type of diet is that your dog doesn't have to eat as much as it would a normal ration in order to receive adequate nutritional energy. As a result, chances are that when it begins its work, there won't be any food in its stomach to slow it down. Dogs fed these diets do not have to defecate as often; a decided advantage in the field.

During hunting season, feed your bird dog twice a day, offering 25 percent of the ration two hours before the activity, and the remainder of the diet one hour following its cessation. Never feed your dog within one hour of rigorous physical activity; doing so could predispose it to bloat; a dangerous condition characterized by the swelling and twisting of the stomach along its axis. If this happens, the blood supply to the stomach and other digestive organs can be disrupted, and this, combined with the pain and shock associated with the condition, can quickly lead to death.

Once hunting season is over, switch back to your dog's off-season diet and feeding frequency.

Remember: If activity level does not justify added caloric intake, undesirable weight gain will result.

Grooming

A comprehensive grooming program for your Vizsla should include routine skin and coat care (brushing, bathing), nail care, ear care, and dental care. Good grooming will not only help keep your dog in top shape physically, but the time spent with your Vizsla will provide it with the psychological comfort that this breed craves. As an added benefit, routine grooming and hands-on attention will assist in the early detection of external parasites, tumors, infections, or any other changes or abnormalities that may result from the germination of an internal disease condition.

Brushing and Bathing

As a rule, if you brush your Vizsla on a daily basis, the need for bathing is minimal. Routine bathing should be performed only on those dogs that are continually being exposed to excessive dirt, grease, or other noxious substances in their environment, and for those canines suffering from external parasites or medical conditions such as infections and/or seborrhea.

Nails that touch the floor when the dog is standing upright are in need of a clip.

If a general cleaning is desired for an otherwise healthy dog, the best recommendation is to purchase and use a mild hypoallergenic shampoo that is designed for this purpose. These shampoos are readily available from your veterinarian or favorite pet supply store. Remember, though, that if your dog is afflicted with any type of medical condition, the type of shampoo used should be limited to that recommended or prescribed by your veterinarian.

Prior to giving your dog a bath, apply some type of protection to both eyes to prevent corneal burns if shampoo accidentally gets into the eyes. Mineral oil can be used for this purpose, but a sterile ophthalmic ointment is preferred. Such an ointment can be purchased from your veterinarian or local pet store.

Nail Care

Examine your Vizsla's nails every three to four weeks and trim them as needed. Overgrown, neglected nails will snag and tear easily, causing pain and discomfort. Also nail overgrowth can lead to gait instability and joint stress, two complications that your hunting dog does not need.

To determine whether or not your dog's nails are too long, observe the paws as they rest flat on the floor with your dog standing. If any nail touches the floor surface, it should be trimmed. When trimming nails, use only a brand of nail clipper that is designed for dogs. If your dog's nails are clear, you should be able to note the line of demarcation between the pink quick (the portion of the nail that contains

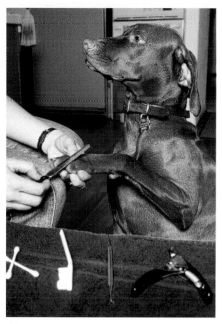

Brushing your Vizsla's teeth daily will help prevent periodontal disease.

Nail trimming is an important part of your pet's grooming program.

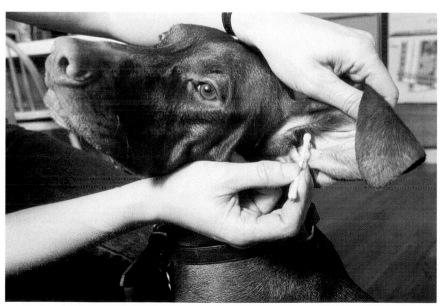

Never insert a cotton swab into the ear canal itself.

the blood supply) and the remaining portions of the nails. Using your clippers, snip off the latter portion just in front of the quick. For those Vizslas with darker nails, use a flashlight or penlight beam to illuminate the quick portion prior to trimming. If this still doesn't enable you to visualize the quick, trim off only small portions at a time until the nail is no longer bearing weight. If bleeding occurs, stop trimming and have your veterinarian finish the job. Although ideally you want to avoid drawing blood when you are trimming your dog's nails, don't worry if you do so. Using a clean cloth or towel, simply apply direct pressure to the end of the bleeding nail for three to five minutes. In most cases, this is all that is needed to stop the bleeding. For stubborn cases, commercially available clotting powder can be applied to the end of the nail to help stop the hemorrhage.

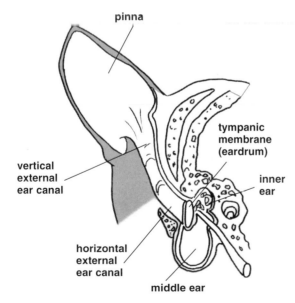

pinna

tympanic membrane (eardrum)

vertical external ear canal

inner ear

horizontal external ear canal

middle ear

Parts of the Vizsla's ear.

Ear Care

Because the canine external ear canal is long, and because the earflaps of Vizslas are pendulous, routine care of the ears is needed to prevent moisture, wax, and debris from accumulating. This involves cleaning and drying the ears on a bimonthly basis. Many different types of ear cleansers and drying agents are readily available from pet stores, pet supply houses, and veterinary offices. Liquid ear cleansers are preferred over powders, since powders tend to become saturated with moisture and trapped in the ear canal. Most liquid ear cleansers contain both a wax solvent and drying agent (astringent) that clean the ear and dry it at the same time.

Before cleaning your dog's ears, take note of any signs of irritation, discharges, or foul odors. If one or all are noted, your pet's ears should be examined by your veterinarian in lieu of cleaning. This is recommended as well for pointers that appear to be constantly shaking or tilting their heads. The reason for this is that unhealthy ears may have torn or diseased eardrums, and introducing a cleansing solution into such an ear can spread infection to the deeper portions and structures within the ear.

Assuming your dog's ears are healthy, begin cleaning by gently pulling the earflap out and away from the head, exposing and straightening the ear canal. Carefully squeeze a liberal amount of ear cleaning solution into the ear and massage the ear canal for 20 seconds. Next, allow your dog to shake its head, then proceed to the opposite ear and follow the same procedure. Once both ears have been treated, use cotton balls or swabs to remove any wax or debris found on the inside folds of the earflap and the outer portions of the ear canal.

Caution: To avoid serious injury to your dog's ear, never allow the swab to enter the actual ear canal.

Dental Care

It is estimated that tooth and gum disease (periodontal disease) strikes over 70 percent of all dogs by three years of age. Not only do plaque-laden teeth and inflamed gums lead to halitosis (foul breath) and eventual tooth loss, but bacteria from these sources can enter the bloodstream and travel to the heart and kidneys, where they can set up an infection. Infection of the heart valves and subsequent heart failure can all too often be traced back to periodontal disease. As a result, keeping your Vizsla's teeth free of tartar and plaque buildup is vital in keeping its teeth and heart healthy.

Even though tartar accumulates much slower on the teeth of Vizslas than smaller breeds of dogs, you should still plan on having your Vizsla's teeth professionally cleaned by your veterinarian every one to two years. Between these visits to the "dog dentist," you should provide at-home dental care on a daily basis. Toothpastes and cleansing solutions designed specifically for dogs are available from your veterinarian or local pet supply stores. For best results, use preparations that contain chlorhexidine, an antimicrobial agent that can provide hours of residual protection against bacteria that may attempt to colonize the tooth and gum surfaces. Do not use toothpastes designed for use in humans on your dog; these can cause severe stomach upset in the dog if swallowed. A soft-bristled toothbrush or cloth should be used to gently massage the paste or solution onto the outer, and if possible, inner surfaces of the teeth and gums. If in doubt, ask your veterinarian to demonstrate the safe and correct procedure for brushing canine teeth.

Special devices designed to help keep your dog's teeth free of tartar can also be used to supplement your efforts at home. Certain rawhide, nylon, and urethane chew bones are specially designed to massage and clean your dog's teeth while it is chewing on the bone. In addition, flossing devices are commercially available that can help reduce tartar buildup more than with brushing alone. Ask your pet health professional for details on these and other methods for keeping your dog's teeth and gums disease-free.

Breeding

If you've ever owned a dog that has had puppies, you know firsthand how exciting and wonderful this event can be; however, bear in mind that the decision to breed your Vizsla should be made thoughtfully, with a full understanding of the responsibilities, costs, and time obligations associated with such a decision. If your dog is a great hunter and competitor, or has an exceptional personality, passing these features into future generations may be well worth the commitment.

A sound knowledge of canine reproductive principles is required before embarking on this adventure. In addition to the information contained in this chapter, be sure to solicit the advice of your veterinarian, experienced breeders, and fellow Vizsla fanciers. The more information you have, the more comfortable you will be with the overall process. Remember that the reputable breeder is responsible for every puppy he or she brings into the world. It is a good idea to make sure you have a home for each puppy before you even breed your bitch.

Puberty and the Reproductive Cycle

Puberty is defined as the age at which female Vizslas first come into heat, and when the male testicles first begin to produce spermatozoa. On the average, Vizslas reach puberty at 8 to 10 months, but just because puberty is reached does not mean that the Vizsla has reached breeding age.

As a general rule, you should wait until your male dog is at least 12 to 14 months old before using him for breeding purposes. Don't breed your bitch until the second or third heat cycle. Even these guidelines may vary, depending on the dog's mental and physical maturity.

The optimum breeding age for female Vizslas is between three to six years. Puppies born to females in these age groups tend to be healthy at birth, fast growers, and relatively easy to wean. After six years, reproductive performance in the female begins a steady decline. While male dogs have greater sexual longevity, this too begins to decline as the dog advances in years.

The Cycle

The estrous cycle is the series of events that occurs within the female reproductive tract between actual heat periods. On the average, this cycle lasts from six to eight months. There are four phases to this cycle: *anestrus, proestrus, estrus,* and *metestrus.*

Anestrus is the period in which there is no reproductive activity in the ovaries—typically four to five months. From anestrus, the reproductive cycle enters the period of proestrus, characterized by increased production of the hormone estrogen by the ovaries, signs include vaginal bleeding and a gradual swelling of the vulva. Proestrus lasts from 7 to 14 days. Normally, female Vizslas will not stand to be mated until the waning days of this phase.

As vaginal bleeding subsides and proestrus ends, estrus, or true heat, begins (the term "estrus" should not be confused with "estrous cycle"). As

Female Vizslas exhibit strong maternal instincts.

with proestrus, this period lasts one to two weeks, and is characterized by sexual receptivity of the bitch to the sire and by ovulation of unfertilized eggs from the ovaries. A common misconception among novice dog owners is that once a dog begins to bleed, she is "in heat" or "on." Actually, she is just beginning proestrus and has yet to reach the stage during which fertilization can take place. Another interesting fact about the heat period in the dog is that eggs are released and become fertilizable at different rates. As a result, it is possible for mixed litters to occur if the female dog happens to be bred to more than one male.

The last stage in the estrous cycle is metestrus, which can last from two to three months. It is said to begin when the female refuses to accept the sire for breeding. It is the period of

uterine repair, or, if fertilization is achieved, the period of pregnancy.

False pregnancies can appear during this metestrual phase. When the ovaries release eggs to be fertilized, they then start to produce a hormone called progesterone. The function of progesterone is to maintain pregnancy if egg fertilization occurs; however, a unique feature about dogs is that even if fertilization does not occur, progesterone levels will remain high for up to ten weeks after heat is over. It is precisely this behavior that is responsible for the condition dog owners know as *pseudopregnancy,* or false pregnancy. All female dogs exhibit some form of pseudopregnancy after they come off heat but, in most, signs associated with it go unnoticed by the owner. Some dogs exhibit marked changes as a result of these high progesterone levels, including mammary gland enlargement with or without the production of milk, and behavioral changes, which include restlessness, nesting, mothering of inanimate objects, and loss of appetite—they may actually appear to be expectant mothers! Often, without the use of ultrasound or radiographic X rays, there is no way to be sure that they are not.

Mating and Pregnancy

As your Vizsla approaches her estrus, you'll notice several changes. First, the vaginal discharge changes from red to brown or tan as estrus arrives. Second, her vulva will turn flaccid in appearance as she comes into heat. Finally, females entering estrus often flag their tails; that is, move the tail to the side when touched around the rear end.

Many breeders begin counting days once proestrual bleeding appears. Usually, by day ten after this bleeding starts, the female becomes willing to accept a male dog and attempts should then be made to breed. If the female refuses to mate at this time, wait two days and try again. After the first mating occurs, a second mating should be performed three to four days later.

Your veterinarian can be helpful in your decision about the best time to breed your Vizsla about to enter into heat. By microscopically examining slides containing smears of vaginal cells, he or she can pinpoint the exact dates when proestrus and estrus begin. This information is especially helpful for bitches that tend to exhibit subtle proestrual and estrual signs.

When your female is ready to be bred, it is better to take her to the male rather than the reverse. Males tend to feel more comfortable in their own territory, and will perform well with fewer problems and distractions.

The Mating Act

The male and female should be on leashes when introduced to each other.

Both owners should be present if possible to reassure the pair and break up a fight if the female has serious objections to the male. If the two seem compatible, breeding can be allowed to take place. Some experts recommend muzzling both dogs before breeding to prevent accidental injuries. Inexperienced dogs may need assistance. Most dogs don't mind the presence of a human, though it may make some uncomfortable. A key point to remember is that once mounting takes place, it's best to leave the two alone. After mounting, the two will lock together, forming what is called a "tie." While intercourse is maintained through the tie, the male may manipulate himself so that both dogs' posteriors are facing each other, with their heads pointed in opposite directions. This is a normal mating position, and tied dogs should not be disturbed until the mating process has been voluntarily completed. Normal ties will last from 10 to 30 minutes, although longer ones are not uncommon. After the tie is released by the male, the two will separate, and breeding is complete.

Occasionally, you will find that some dogs cannot breed properly due to personality problems or acquired physical defects. In these cases, artificial insemination can be used. Just remember that dogs harboring genetic defects that may be preventing them from breeding naturally are not candidates for artificial insemination; they are candidates for neutering.

Pregnancy

Pregnancy in dogs ranges from 59 to 65 days; the average is 63 days. Ultrasonography provides a reliable way to confirm a pregnancy as early as 28 days. If an ultrasound is not available, abdominal palpation by trained hands can achieve similar results but there is much room for error with this method, especially if the female dog is tense during the examination. Abdominal enlargement and mammary development usually become noticeable after the first month of pregnancy. If you're still not sure, radiographic X rays can be used to confirm pregnancies as early as 42 days.

Care of your pregnant Vizsla consists of nothing more than maintaining good nutrition and reducing stress as much as possible. Feed your pregnant bitch a growth-type ration during pregnancy and lactation, similar to puppy food. Vitamin and mineral supplements are generally not required. Moderate exercise, such as two 15-minute walks daily, is certainly acceptable and encouraged during your dog's pregnancy, but avoid hunting and intense activity.

While your dog is pregnant, administer all medications only upon your veterinarian's advice or under his or her direct supervision. Many drugs can be harmful to both mother and unborn pups if given during pregnancy. Always check the labels on products used for flea and tick control before applying to a pregnant bitch. The label should state whether it is safe to use that product on pregnant pets. If it doesn't say anything about it, play it safe: Don't use it. Heartworm prevention medications on the market are safe for use during pregnancy and can be used without interruption.

The Big Day

To predict when whelping (parturition) will occur, record the breeding date and count forward 63 days. Provide your bitch a special area or enclosure, complete with clean towels, in which to build her nest. Allow her at least three weeks before the due date to become familiar and comfortable with her whelping site.

Interestingly enough, the season of the year can affect the time of day your bitch will whelp. For instance,

during the spring and summer months, whelping tends to occur in the early morning, while whelping during the fall and winter months commonly occurs in the late afternoon or evening.

Twelve to twenty-four hours before parturition, the rectal temperature of your bitch will drop to as low as 97°F (36°C). A yellow, gelatinous discharge may appear up to two days before whelping. These signs should alert you of impending parturition.

Stages

Parturition can be divided into three stages:
• Stage One (pre-labor) may last anywhere from 2 to 36 hours. Signs associated with this stage include pacing, anxiety, nest-building, loss of appetite, vomiting, and shivering.
• Stage Two (true labor) is characterized by straining, abdominal contractions, the appearance of the placental sac, and the actual birth of a puppy.
• Stage Three (expulsion) marks the passage of the placenta, either with the puppy at birth or soon thereafter. A dark greenish fluid accompanies a normal delivery.

Don't feel you must intervene in Nature's process. Leave your dog alone in her quiet, stress-free environment. Many dogs will actually delay parturition if disturbed by the unnecessary presence of an owner.

When to Call the Veterinarian

Fortunately, as a breed, Vizslas rarely run into problems with parturition. When should you get concerned about the process? Use the following guidelines to help you determine if a phone call to your veterinarian is warranted. Contact your veterinarian if:

1. your dog's pregnancy has lasted more than 63 days

2. you note a black or red foul-smelling discharge

A basket full of contentment!

3. stage one labor has lasted more than 36 hours

4. more than two hours have elapsed since the onset of stage two labor and no puppy has been born

5. more than three hours elapse between births

6. the mother fails to remove the placental membranes from around the puppy's head (go ahead and remove them yourself)

7. the mother fails to sever the umbilical cord of the pup (tie off the cord with thin gauze or thread by making a knot about one-half inch [13 mm] from the body wall of the puppy, then sever the cord between the tie and the membranes; treat the end of the umbilical stump with tamed iodine)

8. the puppy hasn't started breathing within one minute after birth.

Following Delivery

Following delivery and cleanup by the mother, newborn puppies will usually find their way to her milk supply.

Keep an eye out for puppies that are being rejected and ignored by your female. Rejection may occur if the newborn's body temperature is lower than normal, if it is the runt of the litter, or if it has any physical abnormalities. If you suspect rejection, warm the puppy with a blanket or well-insulated heating pad (use low setting only!), then place it back with its mother and the rest of the litter. If this does not work, you may need to hand-feed the puppy yourself. Contact your veterinarian for instructions.

It is wise to have your dog checked by your veterinarian as soon as you think all the puppies have been delivered. An entire litter is usually born within 12 hours after the onset of parturition (this can vary greatly). A dark red discharge may come from the vulva following the last birth.

Care of Newborn Puppies

As in other pointing breeds, Vizslas exhibit proficient maternal instincts and

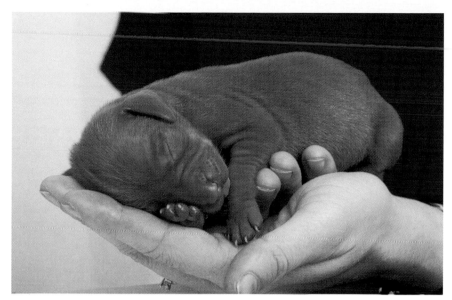

Newborn pups need to be kept warm and well-fed.

rarely require assistance in the care of their offspring; however, there might be instances in which you should intervene. For the most part, normal, healthy, contented puppies will eat, move around, and sleep. Crying usually indicates hunger, and should cease when the puppy is allowed to nurse. If you notice any variations in this behavior, it is time to call your veterinarian.

Formulas

Hypoglycemia (low blood sugar) can result from lack of intake of mother's milk. It is often seen in puppies too weak to nurse. This condition requires immediate attention as it can lead to profound weakness, convulsions, and death. Commercially available formulas are ideal milk substitutes. The amounts you need to feed are printed on the label. In emergency situations, this homemade formula can be prepared and used for puppies: Stir one large egg yolk with enough homogenized milk to make four to six ounces

(113–170 g) of formula. The mixture may be sweetened by adding one teaspoon of honey to 8 ounces (227 g) of formula. This homemade formula can be fed according to the willingness of the puppy to accept it. A rule of thumb is one tablespoon of formula for each 2 ounces (57 g) of the animal's body weight per 24 hours. For example, a 6 ounce (170 g) puppy would get three tablespoons of formula in 24 hours.

Handfeeding a newborn puppy.

Feedings should be performed every two hours. You can obtain a feeding syringe or pet nurser from your veterinarian or local pet supply store. If the neonate simply refuses to eat, tube feeding may be required. Ask your veterinarian for details. It should be emphasized that this formula is only for emergencies, and the commercial formula should be started as soon as possible.

Dangerous Health Signs

Diarrhea is a very dangerous condition in neonatal dogs. Sometimes, the only sign of diarrhea you'll notice is an inflamed rectum, since mothers are so good at cleaning up after their young. Toxic milk syndrome is one of the diseases that can cause diarrhea in neonates. It may result if mastitis (mammary gland infection) or uterine infection exists in the mother. Affected neonates often bloat suddenly, cry frequently, have elevated temperatures, and are restless. When toxic milk syndrome is suspected, neonates must be prevented from nursing the mother, and your veterinarian should be contacted.

Dehydration. A puppy's hydration status may be easily evaluated by testing the elasticity of the skin over its back. If the skin fails to fall back to its natural position after being pulled up with your fingers, the puppy may be dehydrated. Contact the veterinarian if you notice this sign. Since puppies can dehydrate seven times faster than adult dogs, this condition can be rapidly fatal if not treated immediately.

Hypothermia. Another common cause of death in puppies is hypothermia (abnormally low body temperature). This condition is often seen in neonates that have been rejected by their mothers. To help prevent hypothermia, the air temperature should be maintained at or above 70°F (21°C) at all times and care

should be taken to prevent the young from being exposed to drafts and to cold floors.

Urine and feces retention. Orphaned or neglected puppies less than three to four weeks of age have a tendency to retain urine and feces, since they aren't being stimulated to eliminate by their mother. To help orphans perform these necessary functions, massage them gently in the genital area with a cotton ball soaked with warm water until elimination takes place. This should be performed immediately after each feeding and once again between each feeding.

Tail Docking and Dewclaw Removal

The official breed standards for various dogs, including Vizslas, specify artificially shortened tails and removal of dewclaws. Tail docking originated in past centuries as a way to prevent hunting and sporting dogs from injuring their tails while working in thick woods or underbrush. In Vizslas, one-third of the tail is removed in compliance with the Vizsla breed standard (see page 12).

Dewclaws are functionless remnants of the first digit on each paw. Many puppies are born without any dewclaws at all; others may be born with them on the front paws, but not the back, or vice versa. Dewclaws have a nasty habit of getting snagged and torn on carpet, furniture, and underbrush. Infections can develop if this happens repeatedly. For this reason, removal of dewclaws is indicated.

Tail docking and dewclaw removal are best performed within the first week of life. If these procedures are not performed within this time, anesthesia will be required for the surgery. As a result, the procedures will have to be postponed until the dog is 5 to 6 months old and can tolerate anesthesia.

Health Care
for Your Vizsla

Preventive Measures

A complete preventive health care plan is essential for maintaining a high standard of health and quality of life for your Vizsla. By implementing such a program right from the start, you'll prevent or minimize many diseases and disorders later in your dog's life. A comprehensive plan should include at-home physical examinations, vaccinations, internal and external parasite control measures, routine grooming, proper dental care, good nutrition, exercise programs, neutering (optional), and observing safe transportation measures.

The Physical Exam

All Vizsla owners should learn how to perform a basic physical examination on their dogs. Although such exams are not meant to replace routine veterinary checkups, they are helpful for detecting minor or serious conditions in their early stages of development. For convenience, these exams can be combined with regular grooming sessions.

When you take your Vizsla to the veterinarian, he or she probably will begin with an examination of your dog. Watch how your veterinarian performs the exam and ask to participate in the process. Discuss your desire to learn how to do it at home. Your veterinarian will undoubtedly be pleased with your interest and will be happy to help develop your skills.

Assessing Your Vizsla's Condition

Begin the exam by observing your Vizsla from a distance. Observe its general appearance. Watch it move back and forth. Does it appear to be moving normally? An abnormal gait with or without limping or lameness could indicate such things as weakness, nervous system problems, or musculoskeletal problems.

Does your dog stand erect and relaxed? Abnormal postures such as a wide stance with the neck extended could indicate breathing difficulties caused by heart or lung disease. An arching of the back is often indicative of abdominal pain. Note the position of your dog's head. A tilted head is often characteristic of a dog with an irritated or infected ear canal. A droopy head may signify depression and overall malaise. A lame dog might dip its head in response to the pain.

Ask your veterinarian to assist you in learning how to perform a physical exam on your Vizsla at home.

Regular trips to your veterinarian provide the foundation for your Vizsla's preventive health care program.

How is your dog's attitude? Is it alert, active and friendly, or is it lethargic, depressed, or aggressive? Sick or injured animals, especially those in pain, often show aggressive behavior; therefore, you must handle them with caution. Keep in mind that normal behavior will vary among individuals and in different situations. Weakness, shortness of breath, coughing, labored breathing, and, as mentioned before, a wide-based stance could be the first signs of heart or lung problems. A pale bluish hue to the tongue signifies poor tissue oxygenation, often the result of circulation problems. If your dog shows any of the above signs, obtain a pulse by gently pressing your fingers against the upper inner portion of a leg. Normal resting pulse for a dog ranges from 60 to 120 beats per minute. Abnormal pulse or any other signs of heart or lung problems should be reported to your veterinarian immediately.

Taking Your Dog's Temperature

The normal temperature range for dogs is from 100.5 to 102.5°F (38.1–39.2°C). Excited or nervous pets may have elevated temperatures, but a temperature due to excitement should rarely exceed 103.5°F (39.5°C). To take your Vizsla's temperature, use a digital thermometer for safety reasons (glass thermometers can break). Lubricate the tip with Vaseline and insert into its rectum. Hold it in place for two minutes or until the thermometer's audible signal is heard. If the reading is higher than 103.5°F (39.5°C), call your veterinarian for advice.

Weighing Your Vizsla

Get into the habit of weighing your dog every three months and record your readings. Unexplained weight loss or weight gain that is greater than 5 pounds (2.2 kg), or a pattern of continual loss or gain, should prompt you to contact your veterinarian. Such fluctuations or patterns could signify some underlying medical disorder. Vizslas eight years old or older should be weighed monthly, and fluctuations in excess of 3 pounds (1.4 kg) in either direction should be reported to your veterinarian. Also, keep in mind that obesity poses the same health hazards in animals that it does in humans, and can also seriously impair the hunting ability of a bird dog. An overweight Vizsla should be put on a diet and an exercise program formulated and prescribed by its veterinarian.

Checking Parts of the Body

Use a systematic approach when performing the examination on your bird dog. Begin at its head and work backwards toward the tail, checking each body part for abnormalities as you go. A check sheet may be helpful to remind you of each step, and would be an excellent record for future reference.

Eyes: Any abnormalities you may detect involving the eyes should be brought to the attention of your veterinarian. Redness, cloudiness, discharge or drainage, squinting, or unequal pupil sizes may signify trouble. In hunters, it could signify the presence of a foreign body in the eye. Such signs can also be caused by infection, trauma, and glaucoma. The whites of the eyes (called scleras) should be just that—white. If inflammation is present, the scleras are usually reddened. Yellow-tinged scleras (jaundice) may indicate the presence of a serious condition, such as liver failure. A thorough exam by a veterinarian is the only way to determine the cause of the jaundice.

Check the eyelids. Be sure that no foreign objects, eyelashes, or hairs are irritating the surfaces of the eyes. Constant, untreated irritation can lead to corneal injuries, which are extremely painful. Another condition that can occur in Vizslas is prolapse of the gland of the third eyelid, commonly known as cherry eye. This condition is identified as a prominent red swelling or bulge protruding from the retractable membrane (the third eyelid) located in the inner corner of each eye. Cherry eye can also lead to irritation secondary to entrapment of foreign matter on the eye surface. Needless to say, all eyelid abnormalities that you suspect require immediate veterinary attention; left unchecked, they could lead to significant eye damage.

Ears: Inspect the ears of your Vizsla and note any foul smell or discharge. A black or brown discharge could signify an ear mite infestation or a yeast infection. A yellowish, creamy discharge means a bacterial infection or foreign body is present. Other signs of ear disease include constant scratching at the ears, head shaking, and the presence of a head tilt. Because Vizslas have floppy ears, they can be predisposed to ear problems; therefore, plan on instituting a program of ear care to prevent problems from arising.

Nose: Discharges from the nostrils should always alert you to a potential disease challenge. Clear nasal discharges are caused by either allergies or viral infections. A green mucoid discharge indicates bacterial infection, which often can occur secondarily to a foreign object lodged within the nose. Blood coming from the nose can result from trauma, tumors, foreign bodies, or blood-clotting disorders. Visually observe the dog for tumors and ulceration's affecting the mucous membranes of the nose.

Mouth: Gently open your dog's mouth by grasping the head and upper jaw with one hand, tilting the head back, and using your other hand to separate the jaws. The gums and mucous membranes within the mouth should be moist and pink. Pale, dry mucous membranes may indicate anemia, dehydration, or shock. If you suspect a problem, obtain a capillary refill time by pressing on the upper gum with your index finger. The gum region under your finger should turn white. When you release the pressure, the gum should return to a pink color within two seconds. If it takes longer, consult your veterinarian. Further inspect the mouth for swollen gums, foreign objects, tumors, ulcerations, and sores. A foul odor exuding from the mouth can be caused by excessive dental tartar or it could be caused by tumors or infections in the mouth itself.

Body: Run your hands over your dog's entire body and feel for any lumps or bumps. If you think you feel an abnormal mass, compare it to the other side. If you have any doubt that what you feel is normal, consult your veterinarian. Lumps can be abscesses, enlarged lymph nodes, cysts, foreign bodies, soft tissue swellings (such as hernias and bruises), or tumors. The earlier you detect and treat a malignant tumor

Daily brushing could add years to your Vizsla's life.

(cancer), the better the chances are for complete recovery.

Be sure to check for lumps in the mammary region of female Vizslas, especially if they have not been spayed. The testicles of intact males should be examined for abnormal swellings and masses. Intact male and female Vizslas run higher risks of developing cancer than neutered and spayed animals.

Look under the tail for any lesions, masses, or discharges. Observe the region of the anal sacs. These sacs are located at the four o'clock and eight o'clock positions beneath the dog's anus. Normally, the dog will empty the sacs when it defecates, but occasionally, fluid may accumulate in the sacs, and they will need to be manually expressed by you or your veterinarian. If you notice your dog scooting its rear end across the floor, continually biting at its rear end, or having difficulty defecating, it could have impacted anal sacs. Left untreated, the sacs can become infected, leading to eventual rupture.

Reproductive organs: Note any discharges coming from these areas. Not all discharges are abnormal, but some discharges indicate the presence of infections; for example, female dogs coming into heat may have a normal bloody discharge lasting up to three weeks. In addition, male dogs may normally have a small amount of green, mucuslike discharge around the opening of their prepuce. Often, a fetid odor is the first noticeable sign of a problem discharge. In addition, affected dogs often act sick and may run fevers. If you have any doubt whether a discharge is normal, consult your veterinarian.

Abdomen: The stomach, intestines, liver, pancreas, spleen, and kidneys are all located within the abdomen. Gently press both sides of the abdomen just behind the rib cage (some dogs may immediately become tense when you do this). Slowly work your way to the hip region, gently pressing as you go. Unless you have training in palpation, don't expect to know what you are feeling. The purpose of this exercise is to detect any swelling, tenderness, pain, or obvious masses involving the abdomen. If you feel anything strange, consult your veterinarian.

Skin and coat: Evaluate your Vizsla's skin and coat carefully. Signs of skin problems include hair loss, itchiness, redness, oiliness, scaliness, crustiness, and infection. Look closely for parasites, such as fleas and ticks, which can wreak havoc on a dog—not to mention the dog's owner, who can contract serious illness should a tick vacate the animal and attach to the human. Poor nutrition and metabolic disorders (such as hypothyroidism) can cause a dog's hair to become dull and lifeless. The potential causes of skin and coat disorders are so numerous that all abnormalities noted warrant a professional diagnostic workup in order to ensure proper treatment.

Legs and feet: Run your hands down each of your dog's legs, noting any swelling or painful areas. Check the pressure points over the elbows, knees, and wrists for signs of hair loss and/or irritation. Pressure point granulomas (calluses) are not uncommon in Vizslas that are housed on hard surfaces. Finally, check the length of the nails. With your dog's paws planted squarely on the floor, the nails should barely touch the floor surface if at all. If contact is noticeable, a nail trim is in order (see pages 60–62).

With a little practice, you should be able to complete your physical examination in a matter of minutes. Report any abnormal findings discovered during your examination to your veterinarian as soon as possible. The more quickly any condition is treated, the better the chances for a complete, uncomplicated recovery. Remember: Your veterinarian wants to keep your hunter or pet in top physical condition, but he or she cannot do it alone.

Immunizations

Without a functioning immune system, our pets would fall easy prey to every hostile organism that exists. The immune system is designed to protect against such infectious invaders and eliminate any foreign matter or cells that somehow gain entrance into the body. Preventing the growth of cancer cells and tumors is also in its job description. Actual immunity is achieved through the efforts of a complex network of cells, organs, and special chemicals within the body. No one division overshadows another; each team member relies on the others for support. In this way, they all work in unison toward their common goal.

The theory behind immunizing your Vizsla is to artificially provide that initial exposure to certain disease agents that have been rendered noninfective in the laboratory, thereby priming the body's immune system before the animal is exposed to the real infective agent. Doing so will allow for a rapid, effective immune response if this exposure occurs without the lag time associated with a first exposure. Vaccinations against viral diseases are vital, since, as a rule, no specific treatments exist to combat these agents directly once they gain a foothold in the dog's body.

If the bitch has been properly vaccinated before pregnancy, most of her pups will receive protective antibodies in their mother's milk, especially during the first 24 hours of life. These passive antibodies are important, since the immune system of a puppy under six weeks old is incapable of mounting an effective response to any disease organism. Around eight

Recommended Vaccination Schedule

Vaccine	Age for Initial Vaccination	Age for Second Puppy Vaccination	Age for Third Puppy Vaccination	Adult Vaccinations
Distemper	8 weeks	12 weeks	16 weeks	Every 12 months
ICH(Hepatitis)	8 weeks	12 weeks	16 weeks	Every 12 months
Parvovirus	8 weeks	12 weeks	16 weeks	Every 12 months
Parainfluenza	8 weeks	12 weeks	16 weeks	Every 12 months
Leptospirosis	12 weeks	16 weeks		Every 12 months
Rabies*	12 weeks	1 year, 3 months		Varies by state
Bordetella	12 weeks	16 weeks		Every 12 months
Lyme Disease**	12 weeks	16 weeks		Every 12 months

*Confirm frequency of inoculations with your veterinarian.
** Check with your veterinarian to determine if this vaccine is recommended in your region.

weeks, levels of these antibodies begin to taper off, leaving the puppy to fend for itself.

If a puppy that still has adequate levels of passive antibodies present in its system is immunized, the vaccination will be rendered ineffective. For this reason, initial vaccinations for such puppies are usually given around eight weeks, when levels of passive antibodies are low. Vaccination as early as six weeks is indicated in those instances where the mother's vaccinations were not current, or if a lack of passive antibody absorption is a possibility; for instance, inadequate nursing during the first few hours of life.

Diseases against which your puppy or adult dog should be routinely vaccinated include distemper, parvovirus, infectious canine hepatitis (ICH), leptospirosis, canine cough (parainfluenza and bordetellosis), and rabies (see pages 87–88). The first five are normally administered as one injection; the bordetellosis vaccine is administered intranasally or by injection. In addition to the above mentioned, a vaccine against Lyme disease is available, and should be administered to Vizslas that hunt in areas infested with ticks that carry the disease, which also causes serious illness in humans.

Internal Parasite Control

Internal parasites can rob your Vizsla of nutrition, energy, and health. To ensure that your gundog remains free of intestinal parasites such as roundworms, hookworms, and whipworms, stool checks should be performed yearly by your veterinarian. Early detection and treatment of worm infestations will help prevent malnutrition, diarrhea, and stress-related immune suppression from becoming established and complicating any preexisting medical conditions. It will also lessen the risk of human exposure to these parasites, many of which (such as roundworms) can pose significant health risks to people, especially children.

Tapeworms

Tapeworms are segmented flatworms that utilize intermediate hosts such as fleas and rodents to facilitate transmission to dogs and other mammals. The most prevalent species of tapeworm seen in dogs is named

Dipylidium caninum, the double-pored tapeworm. The reason this tapeworm is so common is that it uses the flea as its intermediate host. If a flea harboring tapeworm larvae happens to be ingested by a dog while it is grooming itself, the tapeworm larvae will continue development into adult worms in the dog's small intestine. Dogs infested with adult dog tapeworms rarely exhibit clinical signs of stomach or intestinal upset. With severe infestations, weight loss can occur as the worms absorb nutrients from within the gut. Often, scooting along the floor and chewing in the tail region may alert you to the presence of these pesky parasites. Diagnosis of a tapeworm infestation can be confirmed by actually seeing the white, moving, wormlike segments in fresh feces or small segments resembling brown rice on the hair coat. As far as treatment is concerned, praziquantel and epsiprantel are two effective medications used by veterinarians to eliminate tapeworms from the intestines of dogs.

Hunting dogs such as Vizslas that are exposed to furred game and rodents may come in contact with a more serious type of tapeworm, called *Echinococcus granulosus.* This tapeworm can cause serious and even life-threatening disease in dogs that become exposed to it, and dogs that carry this type of tapeworm can pose a serious health threat to their human owners. As a result, if your Vizsla is known to regularly come in contact with such creatures, it wouldn't hurt to have a stool test performed twice a year to be sure your dog remains free of this dangerous parasite.

Roundworms

Roundworms, known as ascarids or spool worms, are thick-bodied, whitish to cream-colored worms that can inhabit the small intestine of dogs. This is one of the most common

Preventing internal parasites will help keep your dog healthy and strong.

intestinal parasites affecting dogs and young puppies; in fact, because roundworms can infest unborn puppies in their mother's womb or through their mother's milk when nursing, it is estimated that over 95 percent of all puppies are infested with roundworms at or soon after birth. When present in large enough numbers, adult roundworms can cause malnutrition, vomiting, and diarrhea. In severe instances, rupture of an intestine that is full of roundworms has been known to happen. Immature roundworms can cause problems also as they may migrate throughout the lungs, liver, and other tissues of the body before settling down as adults within the intestines. There are a wide variety of deworming drugs effective in removing roundworms from the intestines. You can also make sure your dog receives continual protection against these parasites by seeing to it that its monthly heartworm preventive medication also contains an active ingredient for intestinal parasites.

Hookworms

The hookworm is another type of parasite that inhabits the small intestine of dogs. Unlike the roundworm, which floats unattached within the intestinal lumen, absorbing nutrients through its skin, the hookworm actually uses teeth to attach itself to the wall of the intestine. Once attached, it begins to suck blood from vessels within the wall. Anemia and eventual death result if the dog is not treated for hookworms. The same dewormers used to treat roundworms are also effective against hookworms.

Trichuris vulpis, the dog whipworm, is a slender parasite that colonizes the large intestine. Dogs become infested through exposure to whipworm eggs that are passed in fresh feces of an infested dog. Clinical signs associated with whipworm infestations are usually not serious, and can include a rough, unkempt hair coat, weight loss, diarrhea, and diminished performance in the field. Like other intestinal parasites, definitive diagnosis of a whipworm infestation is made by identifying whipworm eggs in stool under a microscope. Several different types of dewormers are effective at expelling whipworms. Some require only a single treatment; others need follow-ups. Your veterinarian will decide which is best for your dog. Your Vizsla can receive continual protection against these parasites by administering one of the new heartworm medications on a monthly basis.

Other Internal Parasites

Coccidia are microscopic parasites that can invade the intestines of dogs, causing diarrhea, abdominal pain, and weight loss. They are found primarily in puppies housed in crowded, unsanitary conditions. Rapid diagnosis, achieved through the microscopic examination of the stool, is vital to prevent dehydration in affected pups.

Once diagnosed, specific drugs can be administered to kill the parasites. Consult your veterinarian.

Environmental management and cleanliness play a key role in the prevention of all intestinal parasites. Since fleas are the most common carrier of dog tapeworms, rigid flea control measures are essential to protect your dog against infestation by this type of worm; furthermore, daily disposal of fecal material deposited in your yard or near pets' quarters by other dogs effectively blocks transmission of infective parasite eggs.

Canine Heartworm Disease

One important parasite that doesn't live in the intestines is *Dirofilaria immitis,* the canine heartworm. As the name implies, this parasite resides primarily in the heart of its canine host; however, its presence in a dog's body can put an incredible burden on other organs in the body, including the lungs, liver, and kidneys. In many cases, the concentration of these parasites becomes so great that affected dogs collapse and die suddenly. Transmitted from dog to dog by mosquitoes, heartworms pose a risk wherever mosquitoes are found. Because they work where mosquitoes live, all gundogs are especially at risk. Don't be fooled into thinking that just because your Vizsla may stay indoors most of the day the threat is eliminated. Think about it: Have you ever seen a mosquito in your house? If you have, then your dog is at risk!

Although the diseases caused by these internal parasites can be deadly, the good news is that canine heartworm disease is completely and easily preventable through the use of heartworm preventive medications. If your dog is not currently on a heartworm prevention program, schedule an appointment today with your veterinarian to start one. As a responsible pet owner, you owe it to your hunting companion and friend! In warmer climates where mosquitoes are present nearly year-round, heartworm preventive needs to be given 12 months out of the year. In contrast, those regions that experience seasonal changes and cooler temperatures do not require preventive measures for the entire year; only during the warmer mosquito season. Be sure to consult your veterinarian about the proper preventive schedule to follow in your particular area.

Before starting a dog on heartworm preventive medication, a simple blood test needs to be performed to determine if exposure to heartworms has already occurred. If the test results are negative, your dog may be started on a preventive, but if the test is positive for heartworms, preventive medication should not be started. Giving such medication to a dog already harboring adult heartworms and heartworm larvae circulating in the bloodstream could cause dangerous adverse reactions. Also, if you are currently giving your pet preventive medication and you miss a scheduled treatment, always consult your veterinarian before resuming the treatments. Depending on how late the treatment is, retesting may or may not be necessary. For those dogs on a seasonal prevention program, blood retesting should always be performed before the first preventative of the season is given.

The most popular heartworm preventive medications come in tablet form, either chewable or nonchewable, and contain either ivermectin or milbemycin as the active ingredient. In the past, heartworm medication designed to be given daily was the only type of effective preventative available. Although the active ingredient of this daily preventative, diethylcarbamazine, is also quite effective at preventing heartworms if administered consistently, it falls far short of the overall ease and efficacy of the newer preventatives. As a result, if you are currently giving your dog a daily pill, you should replace it with a once-a-month product.

Flea and Tick Control

Fleas

Fleas are the most common external parasites that your Vizsla will have to contend with. Not only can their bites produce extreme discomfort and even allergic reactions, fleas are also host to the most common tapeworm that affects dogs, *Dipylidium caninum.*

To control fleas, you must treat not only your dog, but its environment as well. Your yard should be treated with insecticidal granules every six to eight weeks during the warm months of the year. For your house, consider using polymerized borate compounds, available under various brand names from your veterinarian or favorite pet supply store. Sprinkled on the carpets and near the baseboards of your home, these compounds will kill all fleas that come in contact with them. Noticeable results are usually obtained within a week after application. Best of all, these powders are odorless, easy to use, and safe for pets and children. Under normal conditions, application of this product must be performed every 6 to 12 months. Carpets must remain dry for continued effectiveness; if the carpet becomes damp or is shampooed, reapplication will be necessary.

When treating for fleas on your dog, a number of options are available. Fipronil (Frontline, Rhone Merieux, Inc.) kills adult fleas on dogs and helps to break the flea life cycle by killing immature fleas before they can lay eggs. This product is also effective against ticks that your Vizsla may

Controlling fleas and ticks will improve your dog's performance in the field.

trol. As one might expect, many veterinarians recommend this product only for those dogs that are kept in an indoor (contained) environment.

Ticks

Besides fleas, the next most prevalent external parasite that your Vizsla will likely encounter is the tick. Controlling ticks on your dog and in your environment is not only important for your pet's health, but for yours as well. These unsightly parasites, which attach themselves to their host with sucking mouthparts, can transmit serious diseases, such as Rocky Mountain spotted fever and Lyme disease, to pets and to people. In canine hosts, untreated infestations can also lead to skin irritation, and in severe cases, blood loss anemia. Female ticks lay their eggs in and under sheltered areas in the environment, such as wood stumps, rocks, and wall crevices. Once hatched, the larvae, called "seed ticks," will crawl up onto grass stems or bushes and attach themselves to a host that may happen to pass by. Depending on their life cycle, immature ticks may seek out one to three different host animals to complete the maturation process into an adult.

Since ticks are sensitive to the same type of chemicals as are fleas, treatment and control is basically the same. Thorough and consistent treatment of the yard, and if needed, house, with an approved insecticide is the cornerstone of an effective control program. Since ticks can live for months in their surrounding habitat without a blood meal, treatment should be performed every two to four weeks (as with fleas) during the peak flea and tick seasons in your area. A pyrethrin spray can be applied to your dog's coat prior to a trip to the field to discourage ticks from attaching themselves to the animal. If a few happen

encounter in the woods or field. Applied as a spray or topical drops, fipronil collects in the hair follicles and sebaceous glands of the skin, providing good residual action after initial application. Next, imidacloprid (Advantage, Bayer Corporation) is another addition to the flea control arsenal that can be incorporated into a comprehensive flea control program. Imidacloprid works by killing adult fleas on contact before they can lay eggs. The manufacturer of this product claims that, when it is applied as topical drops on the back, it retains its effectiveness even after shampooing or repeated swimming.

Finally, lufenuron (Program, Ciba-Geigy Corporation) is a product designed to be taken internally by your dog. Available in tablet form, lufenuron sterilizes the fleas that bite the dog. Since they cannot reproduce, fleas eventually die out (in a contained environment) through attrition. It is important to remember that lufenuron does not actually kill fleas; as a result, products that kill adult fleas must be used in conjunction with this treatment in order to achieve effective flea conto slip by, use the same pyrethrin spray to kill those that have attached to the skin. Never attempt to remove ticks from your dog by applying manual pressure alone, or by applying a hot match or needle to the tick's body. Most ticks first killed by the application of a pyrethrin spray will fall off with time once they die. In some cases, you may need to manually remove the dead tick after spraying. When picking them off your dog, in order to prevent accidental exposure to disease, never use your bare hands. Use a pair of gloves and tweezers to grasp the dead tick as close to its attachment site as possible, then pull straight up using constant tension. Once the tick is freed, wash the bite wound with soap and water and then apply a first aid cream or ointment to prevent infection. Again, be sure the tick is completely dead before removal; this will insure that its mouthparts come out attached to the rest of the body. If left behind, the mouthparts can cause an irritating localized skin reaction.

Fortunately, the incidence of inherited diseases in the Vizsla breed is relatively low.

Illness and Disease in Vizslas

Vizslas are not unique in their predisposition and susceptibility to common canine diseases and disorders. As with other breeds, they can suffer their fair share of such viral diseases as parvovirus and distemper, organ dysfunctions such as kidney failure and heart disease, parasitic infestations including intestinal worms and heartworm disease, and injuries involving the bones, tendons, and muscles. It is beyond the scope of this book to provide a comprehensive review of all potential health challenges that your Vizsla may face, but there are numerous excellent books on the market today that focus specifically on diseases and disorders in dogs. Ask your veterinarian to recommend one.

Health disorders of dogs can be placed into 8 categories, depending upon the underlying origin of the disorder. You should be aware that there can be overlap between categories, with one predisposing to the formation of another, or two or more categories existing together.

Inherited Diseases

Inherited diseases are passed from parents to puppies through the genes. Many are congenital in nature; that is, they are present at birth. Others may not become apparent until a dog is several months old. If you are selecting your first Vizsla, or if you are planning a Vizsla breeding program, you should be aware of several inherited disorders. Genetic defects are not especially common; yet, when they do rear their ugly heads, they can be devastating to the individual and to a breeding program.

Genetic disorders show up as abnormalities in either the anatomy or cellular/organ function of affected dogs. Clinical signs associated with the defect will vary, depending upon the type and severity of the disorder, and may affect more than one of the dog's body systems at the same time.

Genetically based diseases can be controlled by neutering known defective or carrier animals. These animals may sometimes be difficult to identify if the defect is not outwardly noticeable, but ethical and prudent breeders, when suspicious that a "bad" gene may be lurking in their breeding stock, will do everything in their power to purge this gene from their midst, even going so far as to perform test matings in order to identify potential carriers. This is the kind of breeder you will want to deal with when purchasing your Vizsla.

When buying a Vizsla, take precautions to reduce the chances of unknowingly purchasing a dog with a genetic defect or one harboring a defective gene:

• Deal only with reputable breeders when selecting your Vizsla.

• Always request referrals from owners who have purchased puppies originating from the breeding pair your puppy will come from, and call them all.

• Always examine your puppy's pedigree before purchase.

• Discuss any questions you may have with the breeder and be sure you feel comfortable with the answers you get.

• Be sure to thoroughly check over your puppy in its own environment, and insist on a physical exam by a veterinarian of your choice.

The Vizsla breed is known to be afflicted with several genetic disorders. Three of the most important include hemophilia A, von Willebrand's disease, and idiopathic epilepsy.

Clotting Factor Deficiencies

Hemophilia A and von Willebrand's disease are classified as clotting factor deficiencies, characterized by a failure in the body's ability to form blood clots in the event of internal or external bleeding. In affected dogs, uncontrolled hemorrhages in and around organs, joints, muscles, and body cavities can occur following even the most minor trauma to the body. Large swellings involving joints, abdomen, and tissues beneath the skin lead to marked lameness and soreness in these dogs. If bleeding occurs in the chest cavity, breathing difficulties arise as well. Cuts and punctures through the skin also result in bleeding that is difficult to control. Vizslas with clotting factor deficiencies are often weak and lethargic because of secondary anemia resulting from internal bleeding.

Diagnosis of clotting factor deficiencies can be made in the laboratory; treatment of acute episodes involves transfusions of fresh blood or blood plasma. Although some bleeding episodes can be life-threatening, most can be controlled through prompt veterinary intervention. Dogs afflicted with this genetic disease should not be hunted or placed into competitive events, as the risk of trauma and subsequent complications resulting from such activities is too great.

Idiopathic Epilepsy

Idiopathic epilepsy, a chemical disorder in the brain, is marked by recurring seizures in affected dogs. Vizslas harboring this genetic predisposition usually start showing signs of this disorder at anywhere from six months to five years, and male Vizslas seem to be more prone to this disorder than are females. Most episodes occur either at night or in the early morning, when the dog is getting up from a rest. Clinical signs can vary widely, and include mild muscular incoordination, disorientation, and convulsions characterized by stiffness, jaw chomping, salivation, eliminations, paddling of all four limbs, and yelping. Following a seizure, a dog experiences a period of confusion and disorientation, lasting from a few minutes to several hours.

Since there are no obvious brain lesions associated with this disorder, diagnosis is based on the dog's age and other historical data, as well as on clinical signs. Treatment involves the intravenous administration of anticonvulsant medication to a convulsing dog. Prevention involves the routine oral administration of the same or similar drug to predisposed Vizslas.

Most seizure episodes are rarely life-threatening, lasting only one to three minutes. In these instances, owners should cover or wrap the dog in a blanket or towel to prevent it from accidentally injuring itself during the attack. Seizures lasting longer than three minutes or occurring one right after another require prompt veterinary intervention.

Degenerative Diseases

These diseases include those associated with normal wear and tear due to age, such as certain forms of kidney and heart disease, but not all degenerative diseases follow the same pattern. For instance, arthritis can result from years of continuous wear and tear on the joints due to hunting, or it can rapidly develop following an acute joint injury. In most instances, degenerative diseases are difficult to treat, with management geared toward slowing the progression of the condition and alleviating clinical signs rather than achieving a cure.

Hip Dysplasia

Hip dysplasia is a degenerative disease that involves the hip joints. It can also be classified as an inherited disease, since genetics plays a role in its transmission. The disease is characterized by a malformation and abnormal articulation of one or both hip joints, resulting in degeneration and

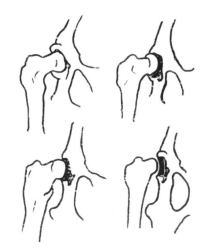

Various degrees of hip dysplasia.

erosion of the joint cartilage and bony surfaces. Although the incidence of hip dysplasia in the Vizsla is much lower than in many of its retriever counterparts, when it occurs, it can have devastating consequences. Hip dysplasia can manifest itself suddenly in the young dog, or may gradually appear over time as the dog matures. In younger dogs, severe pain and lameness can result; in older dogs, a gradual onset of pain and lameness, with restricted joint movement is often the typical presentation.

Diagnosis of hip dysplasia is achieved by radiographing (X ray) suspected joints and from a history of this disorder in the dog's genetic bloodline. Treatment for this condition consists of moderate daily exercise to help strengthen the muscles and tendons underlying and supporting the affected joint, and antiinflammatory medications to help relieve pain. In severe cases of osteoarthrosis, surgical intervention may be required to clean and rebuild the joints in an attempt to restore relatively pain-free function. Also, promising results have been obtained using drugs such as polysulfated glycosaminoglycan (PSGAG) in dogs suffering from the ravages of this disease. PSGAG works to stimulate and encourage the repair of damaged joint cartilage, thereby effectively relieving the pain associated with bone-to-bone contact.

Because many cases of hip dysplasia don't become apparent until a later age when signs appear, several diagnostic methods exist for identifying the disease in younger dogs, before the appearance of symptoms. The Orthopedic Foundation for Animals, Inc. (OFA) has established guidelines for testing and detecting hip dysplasia in dogs two years old or older. X rays of the dog's hip joints are taken by a veterinarian and sent to OFA for review. If no evidence of dysplasia exists on the X rays, the OFA will certify that the dog is free of the condition. Whenever purchasing a Vizsla, ask the seller if the puppy's parents have their OFA certification. It is just one more bit of reassurance that your new puppy comes to you free of disease.

PennHIP is the name given to a new scientific method of predicting the appearance of hip dysplasia in young dogs. PennHIP has been used to estimate the susceptibility for hip dysplasia in dogs as young as 4 months old. Such a tool is especially useful in controlling the spread of the disease, since genetically affected dogs can be identified and neutered before they reach puberty. The PennHIP technique uses X rays to measure the degree of tightness with which the hip joints fit together. Those puppies found to possess a certain degree of joint laxity are considered at high risk of developing hip dysplasia. When purchasing a Vizsla puppy that is 16 weeks old or older, you may want to consider having such a test performed to ensure the soundness of your future hunter.

Endocrine Diseases

Endocrine diseases, caused by disturbances at the level of cells and various organs, affect hormone production. These disorders manifest themselves with a wide variety of clinical signs, and easily can be overlooked as the underlying cause of the symptoms. In fact, many endocrine diseases cannot be detected by a physical exam alone; a thorough laboratory workup is required in most cases to confirm or rule out such a diagnosis.

Diabetes

Diabetes mellitus is caused by a deficiency in the hormone called insulin, which is normally created by the pancreas. Insulin is responsible for regulating the entrance of blood sugar, or glucose, into cells and tissues of the body for use as energy. Deficiencies in this hormone can be caused by any disease involving the pancreas, including chronic pancreatitis. In addition, autoimmune disease, in which the dog's body creates antibodies against its own insulin, has been known to occur. There is evidence that susceptibility to diabetes can be inherited as well. Middle-aged female dogs seem to be more at risk than others.

When a deficiency in insulin occurs, this transfer of glucose from the bloodstream to the tissues does not occur; therefore, blood glucose levels become elevated. At the same time, the cells, tissues, and organs of the body don't receive proper nutrition and have trouble maintaining their function..

Vizslas with this disease will exhibit an increase in water consumption, urination, and weight loss. Complicated and chronic cases may be characterized by depression, blindness, kidney disease, and gangrene of the skin and extremities. Laboratory evaluation of the blood and urine of diabetic dogs reveals abnormally high levels of glucose. Depending on the severity of the clinical signs seen, treatment can range from the simple daily administration of insulin and dietary adjustment to help regulate blood glucose levels, to emergency veterinary treatment and hospitalization.

Immune-Mediated Diseases

It seems ironic that some diseases are caused by the same body system designed for protection against disease, but immune-mediated diseases are not uncommon in dogs. Allergies are types of immune-mediated diseases in which the body overreacts to the presence of a foreign substance and causes an "allergic reaction." More severe autoimmune diseases, such as autoimmune hemolytic anemia and pemphigus, can actually cause tissue damage and organ failure if not brought under control by medication.

Vizslas can suffer from their fair share of allergies, including inhalant allergies and flea allergies. As you might guess, hunting dogs that suffer from allergies may underperform their non-itchy peers in the field.

Inhalant Allergies

Inhalant allergies can be initiated by breathing air containing grass and tree pollens, molds, dander, house dust, and hair. Signs of this type of allergy include face rubbing, licking and chewing at the feet, scratching behind the elbows and shoulders, and symmetrical hair loss. Small red bumps may be noticeable on the skin of affected dogs, and secondary skin infections due to the biting and scratching can occur as well. Because the ear canals of allergic dogs often become inflamed as well, ear infections can result.

Diagnosis of inhalant allergies is made using clinical signs (seasonal versus nonseasonal), response to treatment, and allergy testing. This latter testing may involve actual injections of potential allergy-causing agents into the skin and observing reactions (intradermal testing) or, less reliably, evaluation of blood serum samples for antibodies to offending agents. Traditionally, steroid anti-inflammatory drugs have proven most useful in the control of the clinical signs associated with inhalant allergies, but because long-term continuous use can cause harmful side effects, one or more of the other modes of treatment should be considered. Oral administration of antihistamine medications, combined with omega-3 fatty acid therapy and weekly medicated shampoos, can provide a satisfactory substitute for steroid therapy. Hyposensitization injections containing extracts of the substance(s) identified by intradermal testing as causing the allergy can be successfully given to condition the body to ignore the presence of the offending substance.

Flea Allergy

Apart from the itching and irritation caused by the mechanical action of fleas biting the skin, the itching and hair loss resulting from a flea allergy is a response by the dog's body to flea saliva deposited into the skin. The clinical signs of a flea allergy tend to localize along the back (especially near the base of the tail), hips, and rear legs. Diagnosis is determined by the presence of fleas on the dog, and upon distribution of clinical signs. Flea control is the treatment of choice for this disorder. In addition, the same type of treatments used to control inhalant allergies can be used to help reduce clinical signs associated with flea allergies.

Nutritional Diseases

The importance of this category as an underlying cause of disease in dogs cannot be underestimated. As with humans, nutrition plays a vital (and some say the number one) role in maintaining healthy organ function. It stands to reason, therefore, that nutritional deficiencies, whether caused by external or internal factors, can cause devastating disease. For instance, hypoglycemia—low blood sugar—can be caused by malnutrition.

Hypoglycemia

Hypoglycemia can occur in hunting dogs such as Vizslas due to overexertion and depletion of the body's energy stores during a strenuous hunt. This, in turn, can lead to profound weakness and exhaustion in eager hunters, and, if blood sugar levels are not corrected in time, seizures and death could result. The condition often occurs at the beginning of hunting season and is the result of poor pre-season nutrition and conditioning.

Feeding a light meal two hours before the hunt will usually prevent such an episode from occurring. As an added precaution, hunters should carry a small bottle of honey or corn syrup with them in the field to offer their hunters at regular intervals (every three to five hours) if their dog has a predisposition to this condition.

Nutritional diseases can also be caused by a malfunctioning digestive system. Disruptions in the body's ability to absorb nutrients from their food can have the same effects as if the food wasn't eaten at all. Dogs that are having difficulty putting on weight, or those that underperform even when fed a high-quality diet, should be evaluated by your veterinarian. Detecting a problem early will prevent lasting long-term effects.

Neoplastic Diseases

Neoplasia becomes an important differential diagnosis to consider in any disease affecting an older animal, but that is not to say that younger dogs can't be stricken with this before their time. The term *neoplasia* refers to the uncontrolled, progressive proliferation of cells in the body. Bypassing the body's normal mechanisms for controlling growth, neoplastic cells reproduce at abnormal rates, often coalescing into firm, distinct masses called tumors. Neoplasia can be classified as either benign or malignant (cancerous), depending on the behavior of the cells involved.

Cancer in dogs acts in the same way it does in people, and, depending upon which organ system is involved, can present itself through a wide variety of clinical signs and symptoms. Benign neoplasia can cause damage just by sheer size and mechanical disruption; malignant neoplasia can spread throughout the body and affect many organs at once.

Diagnosis of a neoplastic disorder can be made using clinical signs, laboratory testing, radiology, ultrasound, or tumor biopsy. A combination of surgery, radiation, and chemotherapy is the most favored protocol for treating especially difficult malignancies in dogs. The earlier a cancer is detected, the greater are the chances for complete cure.

Infectious/Parasitic Diseases

In dogs, this classification of disease has the highest incidence of all the others combined. A multitude of viral, bacterial, and fungal organisms can infect dogs and cause disease, especially in dogs that are allowed to roam and interact indiscriminately with other animals and that have not been properly vaccinated. Intestinal parasites are also common in dogs, and, besides causing gastrointestinal upsets, can cause skin disorders, malnutrition, and immune system suppression. External parasites, such as fleas, can carry with them their share of health problems as well.

Selected infections and parasitic diseases are:

Demodectic mange is an example of a parasitic disease that would also fall into the category of an inherited disease, since Vizslas affected by this parasite usually have poor immune function. Characterized by hair loss without itching (unless a bacterial skin infection is also present), demodex usually strikes dogs under two years old that have an abnormal immune system or one that has been recently stressed or suppressed. Diagnosis is confirmed through microscopic examinations of skin scrapings, but a cure can be difficult since the condition is inherited.

Canine distemper is an infamous viral disease that used to be one of the leading causes of death in unvaccinated puppies throughout the world. Although the incidence of this disease has decreased dramatically over the years due to vaccination programs, the distemper virus is still out there and can strike without warning. It is highly contagious and can travel some distance on an air current. Distemper is considered a multifaceted disease; that is, it can affect a number of different body systems, including the respiratory, gastrointestinal, and nervous systems. Coughing, breathing difficulties, eye and nose discharges, vomiting and diarrhea, blindness, paralysis, and seizures are just some of the clinical signs that can result from the infection. In those dogs that do not die from the disease, serious side effects from it can plague them the rest of their lives. Unfortunately, as with other viral diseases, there is no specific treatment once a dog becomes infected.

Parvovirus commonly strikes young, unvaccinated puppies under the age of six weeks, although dogs of all ages can be susceptible to infection. It is highly contagious, spreading from dog to dog through oral contamination with infected feces. Parvovirus affects the intestines, causing severe diarrhea and dehydration. It causes immune system depression, leaving the infected dog open to infection by other opportunistic organisms. In some puppies, the heart can be affected by the virus, leading to sudden death from heart failure.

Infectious Canine Hepatitis, also known as CAV-1, is readily transmissible from dog to dog through contact with all types of body excretions, especially the urine. As the name implies, once the organism enters the dog's body, it causes a severe inflammation of the liver, or hepatitis; however, CAV-1 does not stop there. Other organ systems, including the eyes and kidneys, are often attacked as well. Clinical signs of this disease include abdominal pain, jaundice, and internal bleeding. Another characteristic lesion of infectious canine hepatitis is called "blue eye." In this condition, one or both eyes can take on a blue appearance due to fluid buildup and inflammation within the eye(s).

Leptospirosis is a bacterial disease of dogs characterized by jaundice, vomiting, and kidney failure. Liver, kidney, and blood involvement can lead to intense vomiting and diarrhea, along with anemia and internal bleeding. Dogs become infected with the organisms through contact with infected urine. Leptospirosis is more likely to show up in kennels where dogs are kept together under poor sanitary conditions but Vizslas hunting on land occupied by feral dogs, coyotes, and/or wolves, and drinking from stagnant water pools on such land, are at risk as well.

Canine cough (parainfluenza and bordetellosis) is a disease complex that is found most often in areas where dogs are congregated, such as kennels, grooming salons, and dog shows. The disease is highly contagious, transmitted by air and wind currents that are contaminated with cough and sneeze droplets from infected dogs. For this reason, all dogs, young and old, kenneled and unkenneled, can be threatened. The classical clinical sign associated with an uncomplicated case of canine cough is a relentless dry, hacking cough. There is no one organism on which to solely place the blame for this disease; in fact, over six different causative agents have been isolated, causing disease by themselves or in combination with the others. The two most important of these agents include a bacterium called *Bordetella bronchiseptica* and the canine *parainfluenza* virus. The former can cause permanent damage to a dog's airway if not treated soon enough.

Rabies is a deadly viral disease that can infect any warm-blooded mammal. The incidence of rabies in the United States varies with each state, depending upon the normal fauna found in that state, and on existing vaccination laws. The rabies virus is most commonly transmitted through the saliva of infected animals, usually through a bite wound or contamination of existing open wounds or exposed mucous membranes. The disease is uniformly fatal once contracted. It should be suspected any time a dog exhibits changes in behavior accompanied by unexplained symptoms involving the nervous system. Some of the symptoms include paralysis, incoordination, inability to swallow food, and aggressiveness (but keep in mind that not all rabid animals become aggressive and foam at the mouth). Unfortunately, the only way to definitively diagnose a case of rabies is to have a laboratory analysis performed on the animal's brain tissue, which means, of course, euthanasia of the animal in question.

Lyme disease has come to the forefront in public awareness in recent years because of its ability to cause serious illness in humans. The disease, caused by the bacteria *Borrelia burgdorferi,* is primarily spread to dogs and humans through the bite of an infected tick. Many different species of ticks can be involved, including the deer tick, the black-legged tick, and the Western black-legged tick. Ticks, however, are not the only way the disease can be spread; fleas and other biting insects are capable of spreading it. In addition, there have even been incidents in which Lyme disease has been transmitted by direct contact with infected body fluids. Because of this ease of transmission, Lyme disease is one of the most commonly reported tick-borne diseases, and has been diagnosed in most states across the country. Because of the greater potential for exposure to infected ticks, hunting dogs such as Vizslas have an increased risk of contracting this malady.

Clinical signs of Lyme disease in dogs include loss of appetite, lethargy, high fever, swollen lymph nodes and joints, and a sudden onset of lameness. This lameness often resolves of its own accord, only to recur weeks to months later. In untreated dogs, kidney disease and heart disease can

Ticks can transmit a variety of illnesses, including Lyme disease.

The needs of older Vizslas differ from those of their younger counterparts.

be unfortunate results. Diagnosis is based upon a history of exposure to ticks and of recurring lameness. Veterinarians now have the ability to test for this disease in-house, affording a rapid confirmation or denial of the suspected diagnosis. Immediate treatment of a diagnosed case of Lyme disease is essential in order to prevent permanent damage to the joints or internal organs. Many different types of antibiotics can be used to treat this disease, and acute signs will usually disappear within 36 hours of instituting such therapy. Long-standing infections may not respond as well, and require a more vigorous treatment approach.

A vaccine against Lyme disease is now available for use in dogs and should be given to your Vizsla if it hunts in high-risk areas. After the initial immunization, a booster is recommended three weeks later, followed thereafter by annual revaccination. Tick control is another important control measure to prevent Lyme disease. Prompt removal of ticks will help break the transmission cycle (see pages 80–81).

Vizslas allowed to hang their heads out of the windows of moving cars are at great risk of eye and ear injuries.

Traumatic/Toxic Disorders

Traumatic disorders include not only those produced by direct, external physical trauma (such as a fracture), but also those produced by trauma to an organ or organ system from within, such as poisons and foreign bodies. Vizslas used for hunting will undoubtedly earn their fair share of sprains, bruises, and sore muscles, as well as snakebite, poisoned predator baits, and accidental gunshot wounds.

Caring for the Older Vizsla

Because of advancements in nutrition and overall health care, dogs are living longer than they were 20 years ago. The average lifespan of a Vizsla today is about 14 years. As a rule, Vizslas should be considered geriatric once they exceed eight years; however, genetic, nutritional, and/or environmental factors will determine whether or not the aging changes occurring in the body will actually match the dog's chronological age.

As your Vizsla matures, it will inevitably undergo mental and physical changes resulting from years of wear and tear on all body systems. As a result, husbandry practices need to be adjusted to compensate for these changes. Below is a summary of just some of those changes, and how you,

as a responsible dog owner, should respond to them.

Change: A reduction in the overall metabolic rate occurs, leading to reduced activity and a predisposition to weight gain. **Response:** Switch your dog over to a senior adult diet that is high in fiber and low in calories to help keep unwanted weight gain at bay.

Change: The heart becomes less efficient at pumping blood, causing an earlier onset of fatigue during exercise and hunting activities. **Response:** Maintain a moderate exercise program to keep the heart and lungs conditioned. Keep the teeth clean and shiny.

Change: Joint pain and reduced joint mobility may result from arthritis, and a general atrophy of the muscles of limbs and hips occurs due to decreased muscle activity and age-related protein loss from the body. **Response:** Maintain a moderate exercise program to help keep the bones strong, the joints flexible, and the muscles toned. Keep the toenails trimmed short; older dogs suffering from arthritis don't need the added challenge and pain of having to ambulate with nails growing to the floor. If needed, provide ramps to help arthritic dogs negotiate steps and heights. Keep food and water bowls easily accessible.

Change: Skin and coat disorders may occur due to aging effects upon the hair cycle and from metabolic and endocrine upsets. **Response:** Groom and brush your dog daily. Skin and coat changes secondary to aging, such as oily skin and abnormal shedding, can often be managed well with proper grooming.

Change: The kidneys become less efficient at filtering wastes, and a decrease in liver function makes it more difficult to metabolize nutrients and detoxify poisons within the body. **Response:** Have a routine blood profile and urinalysis performed annually by your veterinarian to provide for the early detection and correction of disorders involving these organs. If indicated, feed a ration that is restricted in protein. Offer your dog filtered water to drink instead of normal tap water.

Change: Fertility and reproductive performance diminish, and the incidence of uterine, mammary, or prostate disease increases, especially in non-neutered dogs. **Response:** Have your Vizsla neutered before its eighth birthday.

Change: The gastrointestinal tract exhibits a reduced tolerance to dietary fluctuations and excesses, and the ability to digest food properly may become partially impaired, predisposing to flare-ups of gastritis, colitis, and constipation. **Response:** Keep your dog's diet consistent. Feed a diet that is high in fiber and easy to digest.

Change: The efficiency and activity of the immune system become compromised with age. As a result, geriatric pets are more susceptible to disease, especially viruses and cancer. **Response:** Perform at-home physical examinations routinely and keep your dog current on its vaccinations.

Change: The activity of the endocrine glands may start to diminish, leaving your Vizsla with hormone-related disorders such as hypothyroidism and diabetes mellitus.

Response: Have a routine blood profile performed annually by your veterinarian to provide for the early detection and correction of such hormonal problems should they occur.

Change: Mental and sensory acuity diminish, leading to reduced recognition, poor appetite, and varying degrees of senile behavior. Age-related cataracts or lens cloudiness can lead to loss of vision. **Response:** To compensate for decreased sensory awareness, approach older dogs more slowly than you would younger ones, using a calm, reassuring voice to further enhance recognition. Consider warming your dog's food in order to increase its sensory appeal. Do not randomly rearrange furniture and fixtures within the house, as visually impaired dogs might become confused.

Continue to provide your aging Vizsla with lots of attention each day. Constantly reinforce the unique companionship bond that only owners of these remarkable dogs can experience. After all, you've lived a life together, and the memories you've made with this loyal friend of yours will be a constant source of happiness and comfort as you grow old yourself. Indeed, that's one of the finest rewards you'll reap for owning and loving a Vizsla!

How-to:
Performing First Aid on Your Vizsla

If your Vizsla is suddenly injured or ill at home or in the field, don't panic! This will only hinder your first aid efforts. The ultimate goal of any first aid is simple: to stabilize your dog's condition until professional medical care can be obtained.

Note: Unless your dog is vomiting or unconscious, always muzzle your dog before attempting any first aid.

Wounds

The two primary goals of wound management are to control any bleeding that may be present, and to prevent further trauma or contamination of the wound.

To control bleeding, immediately apply direct pressure to the source of the hemorrhage. Any readily available absorbable material or object can be used as a compress, including gauze, towels, or shirts. Pressure should be applied for no less than five minutes. If bleeding still persists, secure the compress

Items to Include in a First Aid Kit

- Elastic bandages
- 2-inch gauze roll
- Digital thermometer
- Antibiotic cream or ointment
- Sterile nonstick dressings
- Sterile ophthalmic ointment
- Saline solution
- Snakebite kit
- Tourniquet
- 2-inch adhesive tape
- Hydrogen Peroxide (3 percent)
- Betadine solution
- Tongue depressors
- Bandage scissors
- Tweezers
- Cotton balls

using gauze, a belt, pantyhose, or a necktie, and seek veterinary help immediately. If an extremity is involved, pressure applied to the inside upper portion of the affected leg will also reduce blood flow to the limb. If needed, a tourniquet may be applied just above the wound, using a belt, necktie, or pantyhose. A pencil,

ruler, or wooden spoon can be used to twist and tighten the tourniquet until bleeding has been minimized. To prevent permanent damage to the limb, be sure you are able to pass one finger between the tourniquet and the skin without too much effort. Release tourniquet pressure for 30 seconds every 10 to 15 minutes until veterinary care is obtained.

Once the bleeding has been brought under control, a dressing should be applied to the wound for protection. If the wound is relatively minor and had minimal bleeding, it should be cleaned first using warm, soapy water or hydrogen peroxide. After cleaning, blot dry and apply clean or sterile dressing material (nonstick gauze and clean cloth) to the wound. Next, overwrap the dressing with a gauze wrap or an elastic bandage and affix with tape.

For more serious wounds that bleed profusely, don't attempt to clean before applying the dressing. Also, if a deeply penetrated foreign body is protruding from the wound, do not remove it— straddle the foreign body with the bandage wrap and seek veterinary attention immediately.

Poisoning

General symptoms associated with poisoning include vomiting, diarrhea, unconsciousness, seizures, abdominal pain, excessive salivation, panting, and shock. Common sources of poisoning in dogs include certain houseplants, rodent poisons, insecticides, chocolate, ethylene glycol (antifreeze), drug overdose, and ingestion of spoiled food.

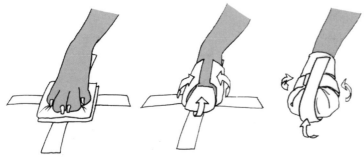

Bandaging a lacerated paw.

The goals of first aid treatment for poisoning should be geared toward diluting or neutralizing the poison. If the poison originated from a container, always read and follow the label directions concerning accidental poisoning. In addition, be sure to take the label and container with you to your veterinarian.

If your dog has ingested a caustic or petroleum-based substance, or is severely depressed, seizing, or unconscious, waste no time in seeking veterinary help. Treatment in these instances should be administered only under a veterinarian's guidance.

For other ingested poisons, induce vomiting using a teaspoon per 10 pounds (4.5 kg) of body weight of hydrogen peroxide or 1/2 ml per pound of syrup of ipecac. Repeat the dosage of hydrogen peroxide in five minutes if needed.

Following evacuation of the stomach, administer two cups of water orally to help dilute any remaining poison. If available, administer activated charcoal (mix 25 grams of powder in water to form a slurry, then administer one ml per pound of body weight)

Dietary indiscretion can easily lead to digestive upsets.

A rolled-up magazine can be used to temporarily stabilize a fracture of the forelimb.

or whole milk (one cup) to help deactivate poison. Take to a veterinarian immediately.

Bone Fractures

Signs of a fractured bone will include abnormal limb position or mobility, localized pain, bruising, and/or crepitation (the crackling feel made when two ends of bone rub together). If the fracture is open—that is, the ends of the bone are protruding through the skin—do not attempt to replace the exposed ends of bone or clean the wound. Control any bleeding that may be present and apply a clean or sterile bandage to the site prior to transporting your dog to your veterinarian. If the fracture is closed and is suspected below the dog's elbow or knee, immobilize it by applying a splint to the affected region. A rolled-up magazine affixed to the limb with adhesive tape or cloth makes an excellent splint.

Snakebite

Consequences associated with snakebite are related to the type of snake involved, the amount of venom injected into the dog, and the location of the bite. Signs include obvious puncture wounds, pain, swelling, breathing difficulties, shock, and paralysis.

If you have a snakebite kit handy, follow the enclosed instructions. Keep your dog quiet and immobilized to prevent the rapid spread of venom throughout the bloodstream. If you do not have a snakebite kit, and the bite is on an extremity, apply a tourniquet 2 to 3 inches (5–7 cm) above the bite wound. Gauze rolls, rubber tubing, belts, neckties, and pantyhose all make good tourniquets for this purpose. Tighten the tourniquet using a stick, pencil, or similar object. The tourniquet should be tight, yet you should still be able to easily slip a finger between it and the skin. Seek veterinary help immediately. Loosen the tourniquet for 30 seconds every 15 minutes (or sooner if the limb begins to swell) until veterinary care is obtained.

Snakebite is a hazard to dogs that spend time in the field.

Useful Addresses and Literature

Registries

American Kennel Club (AKC)
5580 Centerview Drive
Raleigh, NC 27606-3390

United Kennel Club (UKC)
100 East Kilgore Road
Kalamazoo, MI 49001-5598

Field Dog Stud Book (FDSB)
542 South Dearborn Street
Chicago, IL 60605

National Breed Club

Vizsla Club of America
P.O. Box 639
Stevensville, MO 21666

Field Trial /Hunting Clubs and Associations

Amateur Field Trial Clubs of America
  (AFTCA)
360 Winchester Lane
Stanton, TN 38069

American Bird Hunters Association
  (ABHA)
510 East Davis Field Road
Muskogee, OK 74401

National Bird Hunters Association
  (NBHA)
P.O. Box 1106
Van, TX 75790

National Shoot-To-Retrieve
  Association (NSTRA)
226 North Mill Street, #2
Plainfield, IN 46168

U.S. Complete Shooting Dog
  Association
2501 Marguerite Drive
Greensboro, NC 27406

North American Versatile Hunting Dog
  Association (NAVHDA)
P.O. Box 520
Arlington Heights, IL 60006

Other Organizations

The Bird Dog Foundation, Inc.
P.O. Box 774
Grand Junction, TN 38039

Magazines and Periodicals

The Pointing Dog Journal
P.O. Box 960
Traverse City, MI 49685
(800) 272-3246

Gun Dog
P.O. Box 343
Mt. Morris, IL 61054
(800) 800-7724

Wing & Shot
P.O. Box 343
Mt. Morris, IL 61054
(800) 800-7724

Hunting Test Herald
51 Madison Avenue
New York, NY 10010
(212) 696-8250

Pointing Breed Field Trial News
51 Madison Avenue
New York, NY 10010
(212) 696-8250

The American Field
542 South Dearborn Street
Chicago, IL 60605
(312) 663-9797

The Vizsla News
Published bimonthly by the Vizsla
   Club of America
Subscriptions: (908) 789-9774

Useful Internet Web Sites

American Kennel Club
http://www.akc.org

United Kennel Club
http://www.zmall.com/pet_talk/dog-
   faqs/kennel-clubs/UKC.html

The Orthopedic Foundation for
   Animals, Inc.
http://www.prodogs.com:80/chn/ofa/
   index.htm

American Veterinary Medical
   Association
http://www.avma.org/home.html

Dog Fancy
http://www.dogfancy.com

Ingle & Mead
   http://www.vizsladogs.com/home.htm

The Dog Zone
   http://www.dogzone.com/clubs.htm

Canine Connections Magazine
   http://www.cheta.net/connect/canine
   /director/vizsla.htm

Hungarian Vizsla Society
   http://www.btinternet.com/~hvs.
   vizsla/hvsintro.htm

Fielddog.Com
   http://www.fielddog.com/

Cyber-Pet's Vizsla Breeders
   Showcase
http://www.cyberpet.com/cyberdog/
   breed/vizsla/vizsla.htm

Waltham World of Pet Care
   http://www.waltham.com

Glossary

ABHA American Bird Hunters Association

Agility Competition that measures a dog's ability to maneuver in, around, over, and through various obstacles on a predefined course.

All-breed dog show A dog show in which all breeds may compete.

Allergy Exaggerated immune response to a foreign substance.

Alopecia Hair loss.

American Kennel Club (AKC) The organization that maintains the largest all-breed registry in the United States; also governs dog shows, field trials, and obedience trials.

Amino acids The chemical building blocks of proteins.

Amitriptyline HCl An antianxiety medication used to treat behavioral problems in dogs.

Anemia The reduction in the number of red blood cells in the body.

Anestrus Period of time in which the female's ovaries are inactive.

Antibodies Protein structures produced by cells of the immune system that assist in the destruction of foreign organisms and substances.

Antigen A substance capable of producing an allergic response.

Arthritis Inflammation of a joint.

Ascarid Roundworm.

Aspiration Pneumonia Inflammation of the lungs caused by the accidental inhalation of foreign substances.

Astringent An agent that dries a surface to which it is applied.

Autoimmune disease A disease caused by the body's own immune response to a particular antigen or group of antigens.

Biopsy The act of taking an actual tissue sample from an organ or mass and, after proper preparation, examining the tissue microscopically for identification or for the presence of disease or cellular abnormalities.

Blue eye Characteristic lesion seen in infectious canine hepatitis.

Callus A region of thickened skin devoid of hair.

Cancer The abnormal growth of cells; neoplasia.

Canine Cough Complex A respiratory disease in dogs caused by a group of viral and bacterial organisms that attack the trachea and bronchi and produce inflammation.

Carcinogen A substance or agent capable of producing neoplastic changes in the body.

Cardiovascular Pertaining to the heart and blood vessels.

Castration Removal of the testicles.

Check cord A 20- to 50-foot (6.1–15 m) rope with a clasp at one end; used to allow handlers to distance themselves from a dog during training.

Chemotherapy The treatment of neoplasia by means of chemicals or drugs.

Cherry eye A prolapse of the gland of the third eyelid.

Cleft palate A congenital disease characterized by an incomplete formation of the roof of the mouth, often leading to secondary pneumonia.

Colitis Inflammation of the colon.

Communicable Contagious.

Every Vizsla needs a den of its own.

Congenital disease A disease condition present, whether noticeable or not, at birth.

Corneal Pertaining to the cornea, the transparent surface of the eye.

Cryotherapy The treatment of neoplasia by means of applications of extreme sub-zero temperatures to freeze and kill tumor cells.

DA2LPP The abbreviation for a common canine vaccine containing distemper, infectious hepatitis, leptospirosis, parainfluenza, and parvovirus antigens.

Dewclaws Vestigial first digit on the paw.

Diabetes mellitus A disease caused by a deficiency in the production of the hormone insulin within the body.

Diagnosis Identification of the underlying cause of a particular behavior or disease symptom.

Dietary indiscretion The consumption of food or other substances that are not normal components of a dog's diet.

Diethylcarbamazine A drug once used to prevent heartworm disease in dogs; has been replaced by newer medications.

Distemper A multisystemic disease in dogs caused by a virus.

Dog shows Competitions authorized by the AKC that judge how closely a dog conforms to the standards for its breed.

Dominance The psychological and/or physical superiority of one individual over another.

Edema Fluid retention in the tissues.

Electrolyte A molecule found in body fluids that is capable of conducting an electrical current.

Endocrine Pertaining to the system of hormone-producing glands found in the body.

Epilepsy A central nervous system disorder characterized by seizures.

Estrogen A female sex hormone.

Estrous cycle The series of events occurring in the female reproductive tract that leads up to and includes the actual heat period.

Estrus The period of sexual receptivity by the female; true heat.

Exercise intolerance The inability to engage in physical exertion without becoming weak and lethargic.

False point A point usually initiated by a faint air scent or an old ground scent.

False pregnancy A condition seen in metestrus caused by high residual levels of progesterone in which a female may exhibit outward signs of pregnancy, including swollen abdomen and mammary glands, even though she is not actually pregnant.

Fiber The nondigestible portion of a foodstuff.

Field Dog Stud Book (FDSB) A large bird dog registry in the United States that conducts highly popular field trials throughout the country.

Field training Outdoor training designed to simulate hunting conditions and refine a dog's hunting skills.

Field trials Events held under the guidelines of the AKC or FDSB that test a dog's ability to perform the various hunting functions of its breed.

Fipronil A chemical used to kill fleas on dogs.

General Utility Group A classification of gundogs that have the ability to find, point, and retrieve game all with moderate to excellent effectiveness.

Gingivitis Inflammation of the gums.

Glucocorticosteroids One particular class of corticosteroids that is useful in veterinary medicine for the alleviation of inflammation and itching in dogs, as well as the prevention or counteraction of circulatory shock.

Gun nervousness A condition marked by a startled, hesitant response to the sound of gunfire; different from gun-shyness.

Gun-shyness A condition marked by a terrorized, panicked response to the sound of gunfire.

Habituation A type of learning characterized by a diminished response to a stimulus that is consistently repeated over time.

Hard mouth The tendency of a dog to mutilate game that it retrieves.

Heartworms Parasitic worms that inhabit the heart and blood vessels of affected dogs.

Heat Estrus; period of sexual receptivity.

Hemophilia An inherited disease condition characterized by the body's inability to form blood clots.

Hemostasis The ability of the body to control internal or external bleeding.

Hernia The protrusion of an organ or tissue through an opening in the body wall.

Hip dysplasia An inherited disease characterized by the malformation of the hip joints.

Hookworms Parasitic worms that attach to the walls of the intestines, sucking blood and other nutrients from the host dog.

Hormone A protein or steroid compound that regulates specific physical and chemical reactions in the body.

Hunt dead A type of retrieve in which a dog is brought into an area where game has recently fallen in an effort to scent and find the game.

Hunting tests Noncompetitive sporting events sponsored by the AKC that test a dog's hunting skills against a given standard for its breed.

Hypoallergenic Producing very little allergic response.

Hypoglycemia Low blood sugar.

Hypothermia Abnormally low body temperature.

Hypothyroidism A condition characterized by abnormally low levels of thyroid hormone in the body.

ICH (Infectious Canine Hepatitis) A viral disease of dogs that adversely affects the liver, kidneys, and other internal organs.

Idiopathic A term used to describe any condition for which the cause is unknown.

Imidacloprid A chemical used to kill fleas on dogs.

Immunotherapy The treatment of neoplasia by means of immune system components.

Inguinal Referring to the groin region.

Insulin The hormone that regulates the uptake and utilization of glucose in the body.

Intradermal Within the skin.

Isotonic Having the same electrolyte and chemical balance as body fluids.

Ivermectin An antiparasitic drug useful in preventing canine heartworm disease.

Jaundice A medical condition characterized by the deposition of a yellow pigment in the tissues of the body secondary to a blood or liver disorder.

Larva An immature form of an insect.

Leptospirosis Bacterial disease affecting primarily the liver and kidneys of affected dogs.

Lufenuron An insect development inhibitor used for flea control on dogs.

Lumen The interior of a tubular structure.

Lure A device used to teach a dog to retrieve.

Lyme disease A tick-borne disease causing arthritis and other symptoms in affected dogs.

Magyars A nomadic people who conquered and settled what is today known as Hungary and are credited with the introduction of the Vizsla to Europe.

Malignant Describing the uncontrolled growth and spread of a tumor.

Mange A mite infestation.

Mastitis An inflammation of the mammary glands.

Metabolic Pertaining to the chemical reactions in the body.

Metastasis The spread of a tumor from its site of origin to other parts of the body.

Metestrus The stage of the estrous cycle immediately following true heat.

Microfilariae Heartworm larvae.

Milbemycin A drug that is used to prevent heartworm disease in dogs.

Neoplasia The abnormal growth and division of cells in the body.

Neuter To remove the ovaries and uterus in female dogs or the testicles in male dogs.

Nonslip retrieving A type of retrieve in which a dog remains at its master's heel or blind until game is shot.

Obedience trial An AKC-sanctioned competition that tests how well a dog responds to a given set of commands.

Omega-3 fatty acids Fatty acids derived from cold water fish oil that are used to treat allergies and inflammation in dogs.

Ophthalmic Pertaining to the eye.

Otitis Inflammation of the ear.

Palatability Taste and flavor appeal of a food.

Parainfluenza One of the organisms responsible for canine cough complex.

Parturition The birthing process.

Parvovirus An infectious organism that causes severe gastrointestinal illness in affected dogs; can also lead to heart failure in puppies.

Pemphigus Disease that causes blisters to form on the skin and mucous membranes.

PennHip Diagnostic procedure used to estimate the susceptibility of a dog to hip dysplasia.

Periodontal disease Tooth and gum disease.

This pup stays warm on a chilly day.

Radiograph A pictorial representation of a structure or region of the body created by placing that structure or region over special photographic film and then passing X ray radiation through it.

Range The distance that a dog keeps between itself and its master when hunting.

Release cages Pens used in field training bird dogs, designed to hold live game until manually or electronically released by the trainer.

Roundworms Parasitic worms that inhabit the lumen of the small intestine in dogs; immature forms can migrate through the tissues of the body, causing much damage.

Seed ticks Tick larvae.

Separation anxiety Abnormal behavior characterized by anxiety and stress caused by being left alone.

Socialization A type of learning characterized by the recognition and acceptance of a species or group as nonthreatening to the individual.

Soft mouth The tendency of a dog to handle retrieved game gently and to deliver it to its master unadulterated.

Spay To remove the ovaries and uterus of a female dog.

Specialty dog show A dog show that is exclusive to one particular breed.

Staunchness on point Remaining steady on point until the hunter arrives and flushes the game.

Steadiness to wing and shot The ability of a bird dog to maintain its station after a bird is flushed.

Tapeworms Segmented flatworms that inhabit the intestines of dogs.

Testosterone The male sex hormone.

Toxic-milk syndrome A syndrome affecting nursing puppies that is caused by tainted milk occurring secondary to mastitis.

Tracking test An AKC-sanctioned competition that measures how well

Productive point A point in which actual game has been located and is being held by the dog.

Proestrus The stage of the estrous cycle immediately preceding true heat.

PSGAG Polysulfated glycosaminoglycan; drug used to treat hip dysplasia and arthritis in dogs.

Puberty The age of sexual maturity.

Pyrethrin A chemical used in a variety of flea sprays and shampoos; noted for its safety.

Rabies A uniformly fatal viral disease transmitted primarily by the saliva of infected animals.

a dog can track a scent through a predefined course.

Unproductive point A point caused by the residual scent of game that has just recently left the location.

Vaccine A man-made preparation of antigenic substances designed to elicit an immune response when introduced into the body.

Vaginal cytology A laboratory test used to determine a female's stage of estrous.

Versatile Uplander A wirehaired version of the Vizsla; not yet recognized by the American Kennel Club.

Versatility Certificate Award given to a Vizsla that passes all three tests of the Versatility Program.

Versatility Program An event sponsored by the Vizsla Club of America that tests the conformation, obedience skills, and hunting skills of individual Vizslas.

Von Willebrand's Disease A congenital disease characterized by a deficiency in the body's ability to form blood clots in response to internal or external bleeding.

Whipworms Parasitic worms that inhabit the large intestine of infested dogs.

Vizsla Club of America Code of Ethics

In 1992, the Vizsla Club of America established a code of ethics for breeders and owners of the Vizsla. It includes the following points, and provides a compelling reason to purchase your dog from a reputable breeder.

Sportsmanship. VCA members shall always conduct themselves in a manner which will reflect credit upon themselves, their Vizslas and the sport of purebred dogs, regardless of the location or circumstance, and protect and advance the development of the Vizsla through continued improvement of soundness, stable temperament, natural hunting ability, and conformation as set forth in the official Vizsla Standard.

Health. VCA members shall maintain the best possible standard of canine health, cleanliness and veterinary care in an atmosphere conducive to the stable development of their dogs.

Breeding. VCA members shall breed only with the intention of improving the breed by breeding only those Vizslas who conform to the standard as recognized by the American Kennel Club, and exhibit soundness, stable temperament and natural hunting ability. Members shall breed only those dogs who are free of serious hereditary defects including epilepsy, progressive retinal atrophy, Von Willebrand's disease, entropion, and cranial muscular atrophy and who are over two years of age and have been x-rayed and Orthopedic Foundation for Animals (OFA) certified as free from hip dysplasia.

Index